JAPAN'S POSTWAR DEFENSE POLICY
1947–1968

Studies of the East Asian Institute

Columbia University

MARTIN E. WEINSTEIN

Japan's Postwar Defense Policy, 1947–1968

COLUMBIA UNIVERSITY PRESS

NEW YORK & LONDON

1971

Martin E. Weinstein is Executive Editor and Research Associate at the East Asian Institute, Columbia University

COPYRIGHT © 1969, 1971 COLUMBIA UNIVERSITY PRESS
FIRST PUBLISHED IN BOOK FORM 1971
INTERNATIONAL STANDARD BOOK NUMBER: 0-231-03447-4
LIBRARY OF CONGRESS CATALOG CARD NUMBER: 75-127885
PRINTED IN THE UNITED STATES OF AMERICA

The East Asian Institute of Columbia

University

The East Asian Institute of Columbia University was established in 1949 to prepare graduate students for careers dealing with East Asia, and to aid research and publication on East Asia during the modern period. The faculty of the Institute are grateful to the Ford Foundation and the Rockefeller Foundation for their financial assistance.

The Studies of the East Asian Institute were inaugurated in 1962 to bring to a wider public the results of significant new research on modern and contemporary East Asia.

TO MY PARENTS

George and Mildred Weinstein

Acknowledgments

THE RESEARCH for and the writing of this study were made possible by a Foreign Area Fellowship. I would like to express my appreciation to the Ford Foundation for its financial support.

I owe thanks to Professor James W. Morley, former director of the East Asian Institute, Columbia University, for his counsel in the early stages of research and for putting me in touch with those Japanese involved in making and writing about defense policy; and to Dr. John M. H. Lindbeck, present director of the Institute, for his encouragement and help during the final phase of writing and research. I am especially grateful to Professors William E. Steslicke and Herbert Passin, of Columbia University, for reading the draft manuscript and for pointing out ways to improve it.

I wish to thank the many people in Japan whose hospitality, good humor, and willing assistance enabled me to make this study. It is not possible to mention all their names, but I do want to acknowledge the kindness of Mr. Suzuki Tadakatsu, Kajima Construction Company, and Mr. Nishimura Kumao, Japanese Atomic Energy Commission, both former Foreign Ministry officials, for discussing with me their personal experience and involvement in the conception and early implementation of Japan's defense policy. I would like also to express my gratitude for advice and assistance in research to Mr. Matsumoto Shigeharu, director, International House of Japan;

to Mr. Saeki Kichi, director, Nomura Research Institute; to Mr. Kaihara Osamu, secretary-general, National Defense Council; to Mr. Kishida Junnosuke and Mr. Takase Shoji, Asahi Newspaper Security Policy Research Council; to Mr. Sakanaka Tomohisa, Asahi Newspaper, Political Section; to Mr. Ishi Makoto, Yomiuri Newspaper, International Problems Research Committee; to Professors Momoi Makoto and Hata Ikuhiko, of the National Defense College; to Mr. Yasuda Hiro and Mr. Nishihiro Seiki of the Defense Agency; to Professors Wakaizumi Kei and Kotani Hidejiro, Kyoto Industrial University; to Mr. Sezaki Kasami and Mr. Yoshida Shigenobu of the North American Affairs Bureau; to Mr. Noda Hidejiro of the Asian Bureau, Foreign Ministry; to Mr. Royama Michio, International House of Japan; and to Mr. Fujimaki Shimpei, Foreign Affairs Bureau, Japanese Socialist Party. I am also indebted to Mr. Scott George, political-military affairs counselor, American Embassy in Tokyo; to his assistant, Mr. Steve Dawkins; to Mr. Bernard Krisher, *Newsweek* correspondent in Tokyo; and to Miss Nakai Yoko, USIS, Tokyo, for helping me to meet members of the foreign and defense policy community in Japan.

I would like to thank Mr. Robert D. Murphy, former ambassador to Japan, for reading the chapter on Japanese defense policy in the early 1950s and for giving me the benefit of his wisdom and experience.

Finally, I am deeply grateful to my good friend Mr. Michael J. Leahy, of the *New York Times,* for his encouragement and for reading the proofs.

Columbia University   MARTIN E. WEINSTEIN
April, 1970

Contents

Tables

JAPAN'S POSTWAR DEFENSE POLICY

1947–1968

NOTE: Japanese personal names are given in accordance with Japanese usage: that is, the family name first, the given name last.

Introduction

I UNDERTOOK this study of Japan's postwar defense policy because it seemed to me that in describing how Japan's leaders have gone about protecting their country in the 1950s and 1960s, I would be able to write something relevant and useful both to my fellow Japan specialists and to my colleagues in the study of international politics. Unfortunately, these two groups rarely come together, although they certainly ought to. With a population of one hundred million and the third most productive economy in the world, Japan is one of the more important members of international society—the only highly industrialized non-Western nation, and America's most powerful and stable ally in Asia.

The reasons Japan has received relatively little attention from students of international politics (outside of Japan itself, of course) are not far to seek. To begin with, there is the formidable language barrier. Secondly, Japan has not been a crisis area, as China, India, and the new states of Southeast Asia have been. And thirdly, Japan, being neither a superpower, an ex-colonial or underdeveloped nation, nor a participant in regional community building, has not fitted into any of the categories that have been popular in the study of international politics during the last decade or so.

But the Japanese have had to cope with the universal problem of finding a way to survive as a state in the nuclear age and with the virtually universal problem of adjusting to radi-

cal changes in their international power and status. It seems
to me that in their defense policy, as in their whole foreign
policy, the Japanese leaders have shown great skill in coming
to terms with these problems. For as the following chapters
will show, Japan's Conservative prime ministers and foreign
ministers were unusually quick to perceive the bipolar pattern
of military power which has characterized Far Eastern international relations since World War II. They understood very
early that while a United States–Soviet rivalry in the Far East
offered them an opportunity to reestablish Japan as a viable
political entity, this rivalry also posed the menace of a cataclysmic war, a war in which Japan itself was likely to become
a battleground. Their response was first to concentrate on
making Japan an ally of the United States, and then to devote
themselves to rendering the alliance as unprovocative and inoffensive as possible to the Soviet Union. The result has been
that, since regaining its sovereignty at the San Francisco Peace
Conference in 1951, Japan has enjoyed a relatively high degree
of security at an extremely low cost.

   The commonly held view among the supporters as well as
the critics of this policy is that it has been a derivative of
United States Far Eastern security policy—that the Japanese
Government has had few if any ideas of its own on how Japan
ought to be protected, and has trailed along in the wake of
the United States in foreign and defense affairs. It is generally
recognized that the Government has on occasion failed to meet
the requirements of American policy. This is most obviously
the case on rearmament and on Japan's role in maintaining
regional security. But this tendency to resist American policy
has not been explained in terms of the Government's understanding of Japan's defense requirements. It has instead been
attributed to Japan's Peace Constitution, and to the strong
pacifist pressure of public opinion, which has been kept focused on the Government by the Opposition parties and by

elements of the ruling Liberal Democratic Party. The assumption is that the Government would have rearmed much more than it has, and would be more involved in American-sponsored regional security arrangements, if it had not been restrained by fear of an adverse public reaction. In brief, the Japanese Government's defense policy is seen as being essentially passive—an effort to hold in balance, on the one hand, American demands for bases, rearmament, and a larger role in regional security; and, on the other hand, the deep-seated pacifist, neutralist, antinuclear feelings of the Japanese people. As this introduction suggests, I do not agree with these views, and I hope that the evidence presented in the following pages will lead those who do to a reconsideration.

At certain points the argument I have built rests on only one or two sources, sometimes on a single interview. Despite the scarcity of the evidence at these points, I nevertheless believe that it is worth presenting. Firstly, the evidence in question does not contradict the more substantially documented portions of the study. On the contrary, it clarifies them. Secondly, the sources themselves, in particular two of the key men interviewed, were participants in and trained observers of the events described. Mr. Suzuki Tadakatsu was director of the Central Liaison Agency (the name given to the Foreign Ministry by the Occupation from 1945 to 1948), and later ambassador to Australia. Mr. Nishimura Kumao was chief of the Foreign Ministry Treaty Bureau during 1950–51, and then ambassador to France. Their version of what the Japanese Government's defense policy was in 1947 and in 1950–51 certainly deserves consideration.

Although this study speaks well of the defense policy the Japanese Government has pursued during the last twenty years, it is not intended to be a warning against change. Changes in the distribution of power in the Far East, and in Japan itself, may make a new policy necessary. Hopefully, however, this study will contribute to a better understanding in Japan and in the United States of the accomplishments and the mechanics of Japan's present policy, and by so doing, be of help in the formulation of a future policy that will be at least as prudent and as effective.

ONE

꒰꒱꒰꒱꒰꒱꒰꒱

The Geographical and Historical Setting

THE FOUR main islands of Japan—Hokkaido, Honshu, Shikoku, and Kyushu—form a crescent off the coast of East Asia, stretching fifteen hundred miles from the Soviet Maritime Provinces in the north, toward China's Yangtze Valley in the south. On these islands live one hundred million Japanese, who by dint of their energy, technological skills, and organizational abilities have built the most advanced and the richest industrial economy in Asia. Jutting out toward Japan from the continent is the Korean peninsula, a natural avenue for commerce and invasion. To the east, across the ever-narrowing Pacific Ocean, but still 4,500 miles away, is the United States. Directly north from Hokkaido are Sakhalin and the Kurile Islands. The Ryukyu Islands run south from Kyushu toward Taiwan and the Philippines. Southeast of Honshu in the Pacific are the Bonin Islands.

This simple arrangement of Japan, its four neighbors, and the key outlying islands is the geographic setting within which Japanese defense policy has been made for the last half century.[1] The power of Russia, China, and the United States and

1. A case can be made for including Great Britain among the nations directly involved in Japan's military security before and during World War II. Certainly, Great Britain did play a role in Japanese policy, but compared with the United States, the Soviet Union, China, and Korea, it seems to have played a decidedly secondary role. During the interwar period, Britain's Far Eastern naval forces consisted of a small squadron of light cruisers based in Singapore, which were not considered a threat to Japan's naval position in the Western Pacific. What influence Britain did retain on Japanese policy derived from its status as a signatory to the Washington Naval Treaties (1922) and the London Naval Treaty (1931), and its potential as an ally for the United States, which stationed its main battle fleet at Pearl Harbor, and which was believed by the Japanese Government to pose the principal naval threat to Japan. See Kobayashi Tatsuo, "Kaigun Mondai" [Naval

the policies of these countries toward Japan have changed dramatically during the past fifty years. But improvements in communication and transportation have brought its four neighbors closer to Japan, and they continue to be of critical importance to Japan's security—either because they generate the military power to hurt Japan, or because their proximity makes them natural staging areas for operations against Japan. Proximity, of course, accounts for the strategic importance of Korea and the islands. In friendly hands they form an inner defense perimeter. In hostile hands they are a threatening encirclement.

As a result of World War II, this transformation of defensive bases into threatening positions actually took place. Before the war, Japan exercised sovereignty over Korea, all the Kurile Islands, and southern Sakhalin, as well as the Bonins, the Ryukyus, and Taiwan. Manchuria was a military satellite. Further south in the Pacific, the Caroline and Marshall Islands were under a Japanese mandate. The Philippine Islands, although an American colony, were not heavily fortified. At the time, the four main Japanese islands were at the center of a large empire, the edges of which formed a wide defense perimeter. The Soviet Union, preoccupied with industrial development and domestic and European difficulties, was relatively quiescent in Asia. China was rent by civil war and offered a tempting target for Japanese military expansion. The United States was poorly armed and seemed to be committed to a policy of isolation. Under these conditions, the Japanese home islands were in virtually no danger of attack.

And yet, the Japanese Government was not content with this powerful defensive position. In the 1930s it set out to create an East Asian military and economic sphere led by Japan, which was intended to stabilize the entire region and ensure Japan's security and prosperity. Whoever opposed this scheme was to be persuaded to accept it by Japan's military might.

Japan, of course, was not to realize this dream of regional hegemony. The United States set itself against Japanese hegemony in China and Southeast Asia. Japan's leaders came to see the United States as the main obstacle to their success. They attempted to eliminate this obstacle by delivering a smashing blow to the United States battle fleet at Pearl Harbor, and by sweeping over Southeast Asia and into the Southwest and Central Pacific islands, extending their defense perimeter to mid-ocean. For reasons that were never entirely clear, the United States was supposed to acquiesce in this expansion. But the Americans did not, and the result was World War II.[2]

The conclusion of the war found Japan stripped of all its overseas holdings, bombed out, and on the verge of economic and political collapse. Allied Occupation forces, including British and Australian units, but predominantly American and all under American command, landed in Japan itself. An American Supreme Commander for the Allied Powers (SCAP), with headquarters in Tokyo, was the highest authority in Japan for almost seven years, from September, 1945, until May, 1952. The Americans also garrisoned the Ryukyus and the Bonins, and took over the mandated islands. During the last days of the war, the Soviets invaded Manchuria, southern Sakhalin, and the entire Kurile chain. The Soviets also garrisoned North Korea, while the Americans moved forces into South Korea. Taiwan was returned to China, and it was expected that the

2. Japanese foreign and security policy for the decade before World War II has been examined in great detail in a number of excellent studies. Best known, perhaps, is Herbert Feis, *The Road to Pearl Harbor* (Princeton: Princeton University Press, 1950). A wider and more detailed picture of Japanese policy during this period can be garnered from Robert J. C. Butow, *Tojo and the Coming of the War* (Princeton: Princeton University Press, 1961), Francis C. Jones, *Japan's New Order in East Asia* (London: Oxford University Press, 1954), and James B. Crowley, *Japan's Quest for Autonomy* (Princeton: Princeton University Press, 1966). A most useful documentary source in English is Nobutaka Ike, ed. and trans., *Japan's Decision for War: Records of the 1941 Policy Conferences* (Stanford: Stanford University Press, 1967).

Nationalists would soon consolidate their rule over the mainland.

Postwar defense policy would have to begin by taking into account these hard geographical and military realities. Japan's prewar defense perimeter had been pierced to its core, and then inverted. The ring of defensive positions had become an armed encirclement.

Moreover, the purpose of the United States Occupation was to transform Japan itself from a warlike, aggressor state ruled by authoritarian militarists, into an unarmed, peaceful nation, with a responsible and hopefully democratic government. To achieve this purpose, Japan was "demilitarized" and "democratized." The American Occupation authorities ordered the Japanese Government to disband and abolish the Imperial Army and Navy, still six million strong at the time of the surrender. Japan's military leaders were tried as war criminals by Allied military courts and by the International Military Tribunal for the Far East. All career military men were purged from public life. The aircraft, shipbuilding, and munitions industries were dismantled or destroyed, and restrictions were imposed on heavy and chemical industries. In addition, Japan's Constitution was rewritten to include a renunciation of war as a sovereign right of the nation and a prohibition against the maintenance of land, sea, and air forces as well as any other war potential.[3]

Not satisfied that these measures aimed at the military establishment and the economy would succeed in completely rooting out militarism, the Occupation authorities also called for the decentralization and reduction of the national police

3. The purges are examined in detail in Hans Baerwald, *The Purge of Japanese Leaders under the Occupation* (Berkeley: University of California Press, 1959). Occupation economic policy is treated in G. C. Allen, *Japan's Economic Recovery* (London: Oxford University Press, 1958), and in greater detail in T. A. Bisson, *Zaibatsu Dissolution in Japan* (Berkeley: University of California Press, 1954). An authoritative essay on the origins of Article IX is Theodore McNelly, "The Renunciation of War in the Japanese Constitution," *Political Science Quarterly*, LXXVII, No. 3 (September, 1962), 350–78.

forces under the control of the Home Ministry, which had been used by the Government to stifle liberalism and dissent and to organize the nation for war. The number of policemen was reduced from 81,141 in September, 1945, to 40,995 in January, 1946.[4] In place of the centralized police organization controlled from Tokyo, more than 1,600 tiny police districts were carved out, each operating independently, most without sufficient funds.[5]

It is worth noting these details of the police reform because they touched directly on internal security, which, as shall be seen, has been a central concern in Japan's postwar defense policy.

Demilitarization produced the desired effect. Within a year of the surrender, the Japanese no longer had the means or the will to take up arms, either for attack or for defense. But then defense was not thought necessary. The Americans on the State-War-Navy Coordinating Committee (SWNCC) who drew up the demilitarization program did not expect that the Japanese would have to defend themselves in the future. They operated on the premise that Japan was the principal, if not the only, threat to the tranquillity of the Far East. It was assumed that if Japan's military power were destroyed, Japan and its neighbors would live in peace. There would be no aggressors, and so no need for defense. And if the peace of the Far East were somehow to be threatened again, the new United Nations would provide.[6]

4. Shinobu Seizaburo, *Sengo Nihon Seiji Shi* [Political History of Postwar Japan], II (Tokyo: Jiji Tsushin Sha, 1967), 505.

5. Yoshida Shigeru, *The Yoshida Memoirs*, trans. Yoshida Kenichi (Boston: Houghton Mifflin Company, 1962), p. 178.

6. Frederick S. Dunn, *Peace-Making and the Settlement with Japan* (Princeton: Princeton University Press, 1963), chs. 2 and 3. See also the basic policy prepared by the State-War-Navy Coordinating Committee for the Supreme Commander for the Allied Powers (SCAP), entitled "United States Initial Post-Surrender Policy for Japan," dated September 6, 1945. This document is published in full in SCAP, Government Section, *Political Reorientation of Japan: September 1945 to September 1948*, II (Washington, D.C.: G.P.O., 1949), 429–32.

But during 1946, as the demilitarization program was being implemented, this underlying premise began to crumble. The United States and the Soviet Union fell to quarreling over the shape of the postwar world, including the future of divided Korea. China sank deeper into civil war. With the superpowers at odds, it became doubtful that the United Nations would be able to keep the peace. Even more to the point for the Japanese Government, it was not clear under these proto-cold war conditions when or how the Allies would make peace with Japan, or what form the settlement would take.

In these fluid circumstances, the character of the purged and democratized government fostered by the United States Occupation was of decisive importance in shaping Japan's response. It was a government staffed by the same conservative bureaucracy, purged of its militarist members, that had administered Japan before and during the war—a bureaucracy which revered its Emperor, but which was familiar with and generally supported constitutional, parliamentary institutions. This government was led by moderates, men in the mold of Prime Ministers Shidehara Kijuro, Yoshida Shigeru, and Ashida Hitoshi, all bred in the prewar Foreign Office. These were men who had fallen out with the militarists and who had left the government during the 1930s because of their known friendship for the United States and Great Britain. They were seasoned diplomats, well versed in international politics. Soviet Communism was anathema to them. They believed that a Communist take-over of Japan would mean the destruction of all that they stood for.[7]

7. This strong anti-Communist view crops up repeatedly in *The Yoshida Memoirs* and is especially pronounced in ch. 22, "My Views on Japan's Labor Movement," and ch. 23, "The Communists as a Destructive Force." In fact, Mr. Yoshida believed that fear of a Communist revolution was a key factor behind official and unofficial efforts in Japan during 1945 to negotiate an end to the Pacific War. *Ibid.,* p. 225. The similarity of Mr. Ashida's views was explained to me in an interview with Mr. Suzuki Tadakatsu, on March 1, 1968. Mr. Suzuki, a career diplomat who was director of the Central Liaison Agency in Yokohama during the Occupation, was a close political associate of Mr. Ashida during his tenure as foreign minister and prime minister.

If the wartime alliance between the United States and the Soviet Union were to continue in effect, these men knew that Japan could expect a punitive peace settlement, imposed by the superpowers with the aim of preventing Japan from ever again becoming rich enough and strong enough to threaten their interests in the Far East. This was a bleak, austere prospect. There would be peace and security, but for Japan a punitive peace would smell of the peace and security of a prison. If, on the other hand, the United States and the Soviet Union could not agree on a Japanese peace settlement, the possibilities widened, giving grounds for hope and also for anxiety. It was to be hoped that the United States, its Occupation forces already in Japan, would want Japan to become its ally. In that case, the Americans would have an interest in making Japan prosperous, stable, and secure. For Shidehara, Yoshida, and Ashida, an alliance with the Soviets was unthinkable. It could come about only after a revolution or a Soviet invasion. But a United States–Soviet confrontation could also put Japan in grave danger. The two powers might go to war and make Japan a battleground. Or, the United States might fail to see the value of the Japanese as an ally, and withdraw, leaving Japan unarmed and defenseless, at the mercy of the Soviet Union.

The questions of whether, against whom, and how Japan would be defended in the postwar world were first taken up by the Japanese Government in this setting. The old vision of hegemony in East Asia was shattered. Japan, stripped of its empire and sovereignty, was a defeated, occupied state. Its economy was in ruins and its military establishment nonexistent. The question of defense was inseparably linked with the shape of the peace settlement, which was in turn contingent on the future of United States–Soviet relations.

TWO

ⵕⵕⵕⵕⵕⵕ

The Origins and Basic Conception of Japan's Postwar Defense Policy

I

THE JAPANESE Government's views on the defense question began to crystallize early in 1947. The catalyst was a campaign for an early peace settlement initiated by the Supreme Commander, General Douglas MacArthur. Although General MacArthur's campaign was to sputter through the spring, and was to be snuffed out in July, it nevertheless revealed the depth of United States–Soviet differences over Japan, and it gave the Japanese Government its first opportunity to express its views on the peace settlement and the security question.

General MacArthur's 1947 efforts for an early peace settlement seem to have been undertaken entirely on his own initiative. The General had witnessed the effects of the French occupation in the German Rhineland after World War I, and he was convinced that an extended occupation would produce bitter anti-American feeling in Japan.[1] He also believed that the work assigned to the Occupation was nearing completion. The revised Constitution, embodying both the demilitarization program and far-reaching political reforms, had been ap-

1. Douglas MacArthur, *Reminiscences* (New York: McGraw-Hill Book Company, 1964), p. 282. E. J. Lewe Van Aduard, *Japan from Surrender to Peace* (New York: Frederick A. Praeger, 1954), p. 62. Van Aduard, who represented the Netherlands in Tokyo during the Occupation, offers the most complete account of General MacArthur's efforts in 1947 to stage a peace conference. His book provided the framework for this section, portions of which were confirmed by the other sources cited.

proved by the Japanese Diet and the Far East Commission, and would come into effect on May 3, 1947. He had brought into being the institutions and the legal framework for a peaceful, democratic state. Now, the Japanese people would have to run such a state for themselves. No occupation force could do that for them. Finally, General MacArthur was deeply concerned over the condition of the Japanese economy, and he argued that a peace treaty would set Japan on the road to recovery.[2]

The General's economic argument was his strongest and was also most relevant to the security question. The Japanese economy had been brought almost to a standstill by the surrender in 1945, and when 1947 began there was still little indication that it could be got running again. Industrial production was less than 15 percent of the 1941 figure, and agricultural output, which had been inadequate to feed prewar Japan, had declined because of a lack of chemical fertilizers. The merchant marine was at the bottom of the sea, and Japan, a nation dependent for its very existence on foreign trade, was still cut off by the Allied blockade from all overseas markets and raw materials. Moreover, Japan's managers and entrepreneurs, confronted with the Occupation's economic demilitarization policies aimed at eliminating all economic war potential, plus the threat of reparations, were understandably hesitant to throw themselves into the demanding task of reconstruction. And finally, despite the fact that there was virtually nothing to buy, the newly organized, Occupation-sponsored labor movement demanded and got one wage increase after another, fueling a runaway inflation.[3]

In the winters of 1945–46 and 1946–47 the Japanese were saved from starvation only by food shipments from United States military stores.[4] General MacArthur pointed out that

2. Van Aduard, pp. 60–62.
3. Allen, ch. 1. Edwin O. Reischauer, *The United States and Japan* (New York: The Viking Press, 1962), pp. 205–7.
4. Van Aduard, p. 60. Yoshida, *Memoirs,* pp. 204–6. MacArthur, p. 289.

Japan was becoming a burden on the American taxpayer, who was not yet used to such burdens. Even more serious, he argued, was the fact that the social disorder and the despair resulting from these terrible economic conditions were threatening to undermine his efforts to remake Japan into a stable, responsible democracy.[5]

General MacArthur's prescription for economic recovery called for the conclusion of a peace treaty at the earliest possible date—a treaty that would end the blockade and readmit Japan to world trade. He favored minimal reparations and economic restrictions. He believed that with their sovereignty and self-respect restored, given access to raw materials and markets, and an incentive to work, the Japanese would quickly get back on their feet economically.[6]

At the end of February, he expressed these views privately to the United States Secretary of the Interior and to a group of Congressmen visiting Tokyo. The General also sent his diplomatic adviser, Ambassador George Atcheson, to Washington, D.C., to explain his views and his plans for a peace treaty.[7] In Washington, the General's plans were smothered in doubts and qualifications. The State Department, slipping into a deadlock with the Soviets over the German peace treaty, did not think the time was propitious to begin discussions on a treaty for Japan. The War Department, highly uncertain of its military requirements in the Far East, did not want to end the Occupation.[8]

General MacArthur's response to Washington's hesitancy was to call a press conference at his headquarters in the Dai-Ichi Building on March 17, at which he announced: "The time has now approached that we must talk peace with Japan." [9]

5. Van Aduard, p. 58. MacArthur, p. 290.
6. Van Aduard, p. 62.
7. *Ibid.*, pp. 62, 63. Dunn, pp. 54, 55.
8. Van Aduard, pp. 63–65. Dunn, p. 56.
9. *Pacific Stars and Stripes*, March 18, 1947. Van Aduard, p. 63. Yoshida, *Memoirs*, p. 245.

He praised Japan's political progress under the Occupation, and then pointed out that the economy was stagnating and explained why. The solution was a peace settlement and the end of the Occupation. He concluded by saying that he recognized the necessity for continued control and guidance for Japan, and proposed that following the conclusion of the peace treaty the country be placed under the direct supervision of the United Nations.[10] The General's concluding remarks imply that he either anticipated that the Soviet Union would be a party to the peace treaty, or that he was taking care not to exclude the Russians prematurely.

II

WHEN THIS TREATY initiative surfaced, Prime Minister Yoshida was bringing his first cabinet to a close (May, 1946–May, 1947), floundering in the same economic difficulties that SCAP was so worried about. He was not, however, caught unprepared. As foreign minister in the Shidehara Cabinet (November, 1945–May, 1946), he had already put the Central Liaison Agency (formerly the Foreign Ministry) to work compiling a seven-volume study in English on the territorial issue, dealing with such matters as Japan's claims over the southern Kuriles, the Bonins, and the Ryukyus. He thought that the United States might find his study useful when it came time to draft a peace treaty.[11] This study offers a good example of Mr. Yoshida's attitude toward his government's role under the Occupation. He seems to have considered his dealings with Occupation officials as an extended negotiation in preparation for a peace settlement, and he was intent on regaining his country's sovereignty and rebuilding its self-respect.[12]

10. *Pacific Stars and Stripes,* March 18, 1947. Van Aduard, p. 64. Dunn, p. 55.
11. Yoshida, *Memoirs,* p. 247.
12. *Ibid.,* pp. 246–48. Kōsaka Masataka reaches this same conclusion concerning Mr. Yoshida's attitude toward the Occupation, and he considers it one of the principal reasons for Mr. Yoshida's success as prime minister dur-

General MacArthur's call for an early peace treaty afforded the Japanese Government its first opportunity to sound out the trend of American thinking on the peace settlement and the related issue of security, and to make known its own views. Perhaps some light could be shed on the nature of the United States–Soviet quarrel and its implications for Japan.

From the surrender until 1947, Mr. Yoshida and his colleagues from the Foreign Office, including former Prime Minister Shidehara, based their notions of post-treaty security arrangements on the assumption that the Allies, including the United States and the Soviet Union, would all be party to the peace treaty; that the treaty would include the disarmament provisions of the Potsdam Declaration; and that it would obligate Japan to perpetuate the Occupation's demilitarization program. In the event that the peace settlement took this punitive shape, Prime Minister Yoshida intended to seek security guarantees from the United States, the Soviet Union, Great Britain, and China, and to declare Japan's permanent neutrality.[13] Such an arrangement seemed consistent with General MacArthur's desire to see Japan become the Switzerland of the Far East.[14]

But Mr. Yoshida and his colleagues were not at all certain that they could obtain these security guarantees, or that if obtained they would in reality protect Japan. Despite the deep impression made on the war-weary Japanese people by Gen-

---

ing those difficult years. Kōsaka Masataka, *Saishō Yoshida Shigeru* [Prime Minister Yoshida Shigeru] (Tokyo: Chuo Koron Sha, 1968), pp. 4–24.

13. Yoshida, *Memoirs*, p. 263. That Mr. Yoshida himself held this view in the immediate postwar period is clearer in the original, unabridged, four-volume Japanese version of the *Memoirs*. Yoshida Shigeru, *Kaisō Jūnen* (Tokyo: Shin Shio Sha, 1957), II, 109. Reference will be made to *Kaisō Jūnen* when the material in question is omitted or less clear in the *Memoirs*.

14. Dunn, p. 55, and Yoshida, *Kaisō Jūnen*, II, 108, quote this phrase to describe General MacArthur's views in 1947 and 1948 on Japanese security arrangements, but cite no date or source. However, on March 2, 1949, General MacArthur, in a widely publicized interview with G. Ward Price, correspondent for the *Daily Mail* (London), said: "In case of another war we do not want Japan to fight. Japan's role is to be the Switzerland of the Pacific. We never intended to use Japan as an ally. All we want her to do is remain neutral." *The Mainichi*, March 3, 1949.

eral MacArthur's Swiss analogy—many Japanese still cling to it—Prime Minister Yoshida and his colleagues did not consider it apt, either geographically or strategically. They were inclined to believe that the belligerents in another Far Eastern war would not respect Japan's neutrality. Their position seemed to them to be more comparable to that of Belgium than Switzerland, and the fate of Belgium in 1914, and again in 1940, did not inspire confidence in guarantees of neutrality. Closer to home, the Soviet Union's declaration of war against Japan in August, 1945, in disregard of the neutrality pact still in effect between them, deepened Japanese doubts on the efficacy of neutrality as a means of providing for Japan's future security.[15]

The significance of General MacArthur's campaign for an early peace settlement was that it presented a possible alternative to these dubious schemes for a security policy based on guarantees and unarmed neutrality. Prime Minister Yoshida and his colleagues were aware that the United States and the Soviet Union were at loggerheads on the future of Germany and Korea. They inferred from President Truman's New Year's address in 1947, in which he stated that "Japan and Germany cannot be expected to be left forever in a condition of uncertainty regarding their futures," that the United States might respond to the deadlock in peacemaking by concluding treaties with Germany and Japan without Soviet participation.[16] For Germany, this implied partition. For Japan, it held the promise of a nonpunitive if not a generous peace settlement.

Consequently, Prime Minister Yoshida, during February and March of 1947, instructed the officials of the Central Liaison Agency to enter into private and informal discussions with United States Occupation officials on the peace treaty and the security issue.[17] In effect, the Japanese Government,

15. Yoshida, *Memoirs*, p. 263; *Kaisō Jūnen*, II, 109–12.

16. Yoshida, *Memoirs*, p. 264.

17. *Ibid.*, Confirmed in interviews with Mr. Suzuki Tadakatsu, then director of the Central Liaison Agency, March 1, 1968; and with Mr. Nishimura Kumao, who was chief of the Treaty Bureau, March 13, 1968. See also

although under Occupation control, was attempting to carry on diplomatic discussions with the United States Government. The main obstacle confronting it was one of communication—finding out what United States policy was and getting a hearing for its own views in Washington. For the Japanese had no representatives in Washington, and could deal only with SCAP. SCAP was nominally an Allied organization, and officially an instrument of the United States Government.[18] But as General MacArthur's initiative on the peace conference suggests, in practice he occasionally operated like a sovereign.[19] The Japanese suspected that this was the case. They were frequently uncertain whether the policies enunciated by SCAP originated in SCAP Headquarters or Washington. And they could never be sure that what they proposed to SCAP would reach Washington. One way of circumventing this communication obstacle was to exploit the organizational anomalies and rivalries within SCAP.

There was in Tokyo a United States ambassador, Mr. George Atcheson. He was not, of course, accredited to the Japanese Government but was, instead, assigned by the State Department as diplomatic adviser to General MacArthur. Mr.

William Macmahon Ball, *Japan—Enemy or Ally?* (New York: John Day & Company, 1949), p. 106. Mr. Ball was the Commonwealth representative on the Allied Council for Japan.

18. The eleven-nation Far Eastern Commission and the Allied Council for Japan, representing the United States, the Soviet Union, the Commonwealth, and China, were established at the Moscow Conference in December, 1945, and were granted supervisory powers over SCAP. According to the Moscow Agreement, however, the United States retained a veto in the Commission and was empowered to issue interim directives to SCAP in lieu of Commission directives to the contrary. See "Agreement of Foreign Ministers at Moscow on Establishing Far Eastern Commission and Allied Council for Japan, December 27, 1945," *United States Treaties and Other International Agreements*, II, 1137. Moreover, the Supreme Commander for the Allied Powers was also Commander of the United States Occupation Forces in Japan, and as such received orders from the United States Government through the War Department. See Herbert Feis, *Contest over Japan* (New York: W. W. Norton and Company, 1967), pp. 107–11.

19. This point is made most strongly in George F. Kennan, *Memoirs, 1925–1950* (Boston: Little, Brown and Company, 1967), pp. 368–93. See also Van Aduard, p. 65. Van Aduard hints at this view, as do Yoshida, Dunn, and almost every other writer on the occupation of Japan.

Atcheson traveled frequently to Washington and provided a direct link with the Department of State. Another channel of communication was kept open by Lieutenant General Robert L. Eichelberger, commander of the Eighth Army, whose headquarters was in Yokohama. General Eichelberger also enjoyed a degree of autonomy and was able to communicate directly with the War Department. Mr. Yoshida and Mr. Ashida were friendly with him, and as shall be seen, they sought his advice and assistance.

III

THE JAPANESE diplomats, following Prime Minister Yoshida's instructions, began making discreet, informal inquiries on the peace settlement and security issues. They found the Americans willing to discuss their views, to a point, and also ready to listen. Yoshida writes:

It seemed at the time, however, that the United States Government did not have a clear conception of a post-peace treaty security arrangement for Japan. For instance, Ambassador George Atcheson, the United States representative on the Allied Council, privately told the Japanese diplomats: "The question of Japanese security policy has not yet become a realistic issue. But it seems to me that, when it does, the United States may suggest that Japan request a security guarantee from the United Nations." [20]

Ambassador Atcheson's remarks were consistent with General MacArthur's peace plans, which envisioned United Nations supervision of the peace settlement, but they gave little indication of the variety of plans being hatched in Washington. Within the State Department, a committee headed by Dr. Hugh Borton was drafting a peace treaty under instructions from Secretary of State James Byrnes. This draft treaty was intended to make possible a United States–Soviet agreement

20. Yoshida, *Kaisō Jūnen*, II, 111. This and subsequent quotations from *Kaisō Jūnen* were translated by the writer. The gist of this statement was also confirmed in interviews with Suzuki and Nishimura.

on Japan.[21] It forbade Japan to rearm for twenty-five years, and placed the Japanese Government and economy under Allied supervision and surveillance. Moving on an entirely different tack was Mr. George Kennan, who was at that time establishing the Policy Planning Staff to formulate cold war strategy. The Policy Planning Staff was preoccupied with Germany and Europe during the spring, but it was implicit in Mr. Kennan's views that cooperation with the Soviets was unlikely, and that American policy should be to prevent Japan from falling under Soviet control.[22] Over in the War and Navy Departments the prevailing opinion also ran counter to General MacArthur's. Rather than conclude an early peace and end the Occupation, the War Department preferred to continue the Occupation in order to give the United States the greatest possible freedom in using Japan as a base for military operations in the Far East.[23]

Although unaware of the crosscurrents in Washington, the Japanese diplomats in Tokyo disagreed with Ambassador Atcheson's approach to the security issue. According to Yoshida, they argued as follows:

For Japan, the security issue is an extremely realistic and serious problem. It is not clear that the United Nations peace-keeping machinery will materialize. In any case, it is not now complete and there seems to be no way for Japan to provide for defense against foreign invasion and to protect her independence, except by an alliance with a third power.[24]

Mr. Yoshida indicates in his memoirs that there was no doubt that the "third power" was the United States. His diplomats were trying to find out if the United States Government was really preparing to make a peace settlement without Soviet participation, and if so, whether the United States was

21. Dunn, pp. 57, 58.
22. *Ibid.*, pp. 59–61. See also Kennan, *Memoirs*, pp. 368–96.
23. Dunn, pp. 56, 57.
24. Yoshida, *Kaisō Jūnen*, II, 111, 112. Also interviews with Suzuki and Nishimura.

ready to help defend Japan from the Soviets after making a separate peace. Mr. Yoshida was not proposing a separate peace, but he wanted the United States Government to know that his Government was amenable to such a settlement if it included appropriate arrangements for Japan's security.[25]

By April, 1947, the month in which Mr. Yoshida's party was defeated in general elections and in which the United States Government announced the Truman Doctrine, the concept of a cold war peace settlement had taken firm root in the Japanese Government. Although the new cabinet was a coalition of Socialists and Democrats headed by Mr. Katayama Tetsu, Japan's only Socialist prime minister to date, the security discussions with the United States continued along the lines set by Mr. Yoshida. The leaders of the Socialist Party had not yet given much thought to the security issue, and Prime Minister Katayama was content to have Foreign Minister Ashida Hitoshi tend to that issue while his government concentrated on economic and domestic political problems.[26] Mr. Ashida was a leader of the Democratic Party—a conservative party—and although he and Mr. Yoshida were rivals in domestic politics, they sprang from the same Anglo-American faction in the Foreign Office, and held basically similar views at this time on foreign and defense policy.[27]

During May, when the Katayama coalition cabinet was being formed, both Assistant Secretary of State Dean Acheson and former President Herbert Hoover made public statements

25. Interviews with Suzuki and Nishimura.
26. Interview with Suzuki. Mr. Ashida, a leader in the Democratic Party and a former diplomat, took the post of foreign minister in the coalition cabinet with the understanding that he would be given considerable latitude in the performance of his duties. Moreover, it should be kept in mind that in 1947 Japan had no diplomatic representatives abroad, and no formal foreign relations. The Foreign Minister's powers were narrowly circumscribed. In his study of the Socialist Party's foreign policy program, Arthur Stockwin concludes that prior to December, 1949, when the party announced its advocacy of "permanent neutrality," it did not have a well-defined position on foreign policy. Arthur Stockwin, *The Japanese Socialist Party and Neutralism* (London: Cambridge University Press, 1968), p. 31.
27. Interview with Suzuki.

favoring a separate peace with Japan, if the Soviet Union continued its obstructionist tactics. It was not clear how the Soviets were reacting to General MacArthur's call for a peace conference, but Foreign Minister Ashida picked up where Prime Minister Yoshida had left off, and continued to sound out the Americans. He kept Mr. Yoshida informed of his efforts and several times discussed policy with him.[28] In June, Foreign Minister Ashida decided to go beyond the oral, informal soundings and to put his views on the peace treaty and the security question into a more official, written form. It appeared that the United States Government in Washington was not getting Prime Minister Yoshida's earlier oral messages through SCAP. Perhaps a memorandum on the subject would evoke a more definite response.[29]

On June 28, after conferring with Prime Minister Katayama, Foreign Minister Ashida submitted a document setting forth the Japanese Government's views on the peace treaty and post-treaty security arrangements to Ambassador Atcheson and to Brigadier General Courtney A. Whitney, chief of SCAP's Government Section. General Whitney returned this document the next day with a note to the effect that SCAP considered the time inappropriate to discuss with the Japanese Government the issues raised in its memorandum.[30] On August 17, Ambassador Atcheson, presumably carrying Foreign Minister Ashida's memorandum with him, was killed in an airplane crash on his way back to Washington. Thus, the first attempt by the Japanese Government to convey its views in writing to the United States Government on post-peace treaty security arrangements was stymied.

28. *Ibid.*
29. *Ibid.*
30. Yoshida, *Kaisō Jūnen,* II, 112. Also Suzuki interview. There is no mention of Foreign Minister Ashida's memorandum on post-peace treaty security arrangements, nor is there any reference to this specific incident in General Courtney Whitney's *MacArthur: His Rendezvous with History* (New York: Alfred A. Knopf, 1956).

IV

MEANWHILE, during July, General MacArthur's campaign for a peace conference was snuffed out. Following his press conference on March 22, the State Department and the War Department, although opposed to the General's plans, had reluctantly echoed his call for an early Japanese peace settlement. Plans were made in Washington to hold a peace conference among the eleven member nations of the Far Eastern Commission. The State Department issued invitations early in July. On the 14th, the Soviets publicly declined to attend, and announced that the Japanese peace treaty would have to be dealt with by another Big Four conference, similar to the one that was deadlocked on the German peace treaty. The Chinese Government also favored a Big Four conference on Japan. The Commonwealth nations favored the eleven-nation conference, but they were planning to meet in Canberra in August to discuss Japan, and they wanted the peace conference postponed. The result was no peace conference at all and a further deterioration in United States–Soviet relations, which were also growing increasingly strained in Europe, following the abrupt departure of the Soviet delegation from the Marshall Plan conference in Paris late in June.

The interaction of General MacArthur's peace initiative, the Japanese Government's attempts to widen its foreign policy alternatives, and the growing differences between the United States and Soviet Governments is intricate in detail, but clear in outline. The General's initiative failed primarily because of the widening global split between the superpowers, and at the same time it contributed to that split. In the course of the spring, it became clear to the Japanese Government that United States–Soviet tensions were likely to prevent a general peace conference and might save Japan from a punitive peace settlement. But the Japanese also saw that a United States–Soviet split and a separate peace with the United States would probably turn the Soviets against them, and in the event a separate peace did become possible, they wanted an American guarantee of Japan's security. Thus, the final failure in July of General MacArthur's peace initiative did not dampen Foreign Minister Ashida's concern on the question of post-peace treaty security arrangements. On the contrary, it led the Foreign Minister to make another attempt to communicate with the United States Government on the security question.

In September, Foreign Minister Ashida, with the cooperation of Chief Cabinet Secretary Nishio Suehiro (a Socialist, later the leader of the Democratic-Socialist Party), wrote another memorandum on the security issue for presentation to the United States Government. This memorandum was prepared in the name of Mr. Suzuki Tadakatsu, director of the Central Liaison Agency, who also participated in the wording of the final draft. On September 10, Mr. Suzuki personally handed this memorandum to General Eichelberger, with whom he was on friendly terms. General Eichelberger was about to fly back to the United States on home leave, and Foreign Minister Ashida and Mr. Suzuki understood that while in Washington the General would see to it that Mr. Ashida's memorandum was brought to the attention of the War Department.[31] According to Yoshida:

This memorandum, after stating that the Japanese Government itself would be able to suppress any internal riots or disorders, went on to say:

"At this time of growing international insecurity, the Japanese

31. Robert L. Eichelberger, unpublished diary, by permission of Manuscript Department, William R. Perkins Library, Duke University. In his entry for September 10, 1947, General Eichelberger also made reference to the earlier version of the memorandum that was given to General Whitney in June. Yoshida, *Kaisō Jūnen*, II, 113, 114. Also Suzuki interview. In a letter dated August 22, 1968, General Clovis E. Byers, U.S. Army (retired), who was Chief of Staff of the Eighth Army during 1947, advised me: "I do not remember ever having seen the basic document, but I do remember the general understanding and planning in consonance with the Japanese version which you have quoted. . . . I question that the accuracy of your dissertation would be enhanced by anything that you might acquire from studying the English version."

Government, as the most desirable means of protecting Japan's independence, wishes to enter into a special agreement with the United States against external aggression by a third power; and at the same time, to build up its domestic police forces, on the ground and on the sea. Until the United Nations shows that it can perform the functions set forth in the Charter, we believe that it is the wish of the Japanese people to have Japan's security guaranteed by the United States."

This document was based on the idea that the United States would maintain armed forces in the areas *adjacent* to Japan, and that Japan would maintain bases within the country to be made available for use by the United States forces in an emergency.[32]

Mr. Suzuki met General Eichelberger soon after he returned from his home leave, and he asked him about the reaction in Washington to Foreign Minister Ashida's memorandum. The General's reply indicated to Mr. Suzuki that for the time being the United States was not ready to conclude separate peace treaties with its recent enemies, Germany and Japan.[33] Despite the public statements of President Truman and Assistant Secretary of State Acheson, and despite the Truman Doctrine, the prevailing view in Washington was that the making of peace treaties without Soviet participation would end all hope for a general accord with the Soviets, and the United States

32. Yoshida, *Kaisō Jūnen*, II, 114. Italics added. Mr. Suzuki was involved in the final preparation of this memorandum and remembered well the document and its background. He explained that it was originally written in English, and he was kind enough to read and correct my translation from Japanese back into English. He gave special care to the sentence concerning the stationing of forces and the maintenance of bases. Mr. Suzuki stated that the memorandum explicitly proposed the stationing of U.S. forces in the *areas adjacent to Japan,* which included the Ryukyus and the Bonins, but not in Japan itself; and the maintenance of *emergency-use bases* in Japan by the Japanese Government.

Mr. Nishimura was also well acquainted with the memorandum and thought that this translation was correct.

Mr. Yoshida Kenichi's translation (*Memoirs,* p. 265) is rendered into more graceful English, but omits this sentence. In a telephone interview on June 6, 1968, Professor Yoshida said that he made his abridged translation from the text of *Kaisō Jūnen,* and that he was not acquainted with the original memorandum. It should be noted that neither the Japanese nor the American government was able to make a copy of the Ashida Memorandum available to the writer, and that the above analysis is based on a reconstruction of its content.

33. Interview with Suzuki.

Government still held to the belief that a *modus vivendi* with the Soviets offered the best hope for a stable and peaceful postwar world.

In his memorandum, Foreign Minister Ashida was saying that Japan was ready to cast its lot with the United States in the cold war. In return, he was suggesting that the United States guarantee Japan against a Soviet attack or invasion. But Mr. Ashida was not proposing that the United States assume complete responsibility for Japan's security. He was, rather, asking the United States to guard Japan's external security, while his government took care of internal security. Japan, demilitarized and economically prostrate, could not be expected, for the foreseeable future, to build military forces capable of repelling a Soviet attack. The Government would have all it could do to "build up its domestic police forces, on the ground and on the sea," in order to protect Japan against insurrection and infiltration. It is important to note that, from the Japanese Government's point of view, this sharing of the security burden was intended to give the proposed "special agreement" a mutual, reciprocal character.[34] The Japanese seem to have believed that Japan's strategic value to the United States, their willingness to assume complete responsibility for the internal Communist threat, and their desire to cooperate with the United States in defending Japan against a direct Soviet attack constituted a realistic and reasonable basis for a mutual defense arrangement. Foreign Minister Ashida, and Prime Minister Yoshida before him, were planning to provide for Japan's security by becoming an ally of the United States, not a military dependency.

V

THIS WAS a novel approach. In most alliances, the parties undertake to assist each other in the event one of them is

34. *Ibid.* Also interview with Nishimura.

attacked by a third power. The *quid pro quo* is obvious. In Foreign Minister Ashida's memorandum, the *quid pro quo* is not quite so apparent. It is worthwhile to analyze the memorandum more closely.

The idea that a mutual security agreement might be made with the United States on the basis of this memorandum rested on three related premises. The first premise was that the United States–Soviet split would not be patched up, at least not in the Far East. If it were, the United States would not conclude an alliance with Japan that would be interpreted as being directed against the Soviet Union. This premise could only be tested by the future course of United States–Soviet relations.

The second premise was that the United States Government would judge the defense of Japan to be essential to the security of the United States and would, in its own interests, want to keep United States forces near Japan, probably on Okinawa and the Bonins, and would welcome the opportunity to use bases in Japan itself to repel a Soviet attack. The correctness of this premise depended entirely on the judgment of the United States Government. It alone would decide whether the defense of Japan was vital to American security, and if it was, how best to position its forces to protect Japan.

The third premise, which assumed the correctness of the first two, was that the possibility of a Communist take-over from within, encouraged and assisted by the Soviets, posed a real threat to Japan. If it did, it followed that by assuming responsibility for internal security the Japanese Government would be making a solid contribution to Japan's defense, and therefore to the defense of the United States as well. But was this internal security–external security equation based on actual conditions? Or was it a diplomatic gesture, or perhaps a device for once again making Japan into a police state, or a great military power? In short, did there actually appear to be a serious threat of a Communist take-over from within?

And if so, was it comparable to the threat of direct Soviet aggression?

This last premise and the questions it raises are especially relevant. They touch directly on the mutuality of the defense arrangement sought by the Japanese Government, as well as on its estimates of what the threats were to Japan's national security. Defense policy, briefly defined, is the military, diplomatic, and economic measures taken by a government to protect national security. The need for such measures derives from the belief that there exists a *threat* or *threats*, and the first and most basic step in formulating defense policy is to identify and evaluate these threats.

It is, of course, impossible to measure quantitatively a threat, be it external or internal. Looking first at the external threat, one cannot say that the probability that the Soviet Union would have invaded Japan or bombed its cities under conditions X, Y, or Z was 20, 50, or 90 percent. It was not possible to make such a measurement in 1947, and it is not possible now. One can only evaluate Soviet *capabilities*, make a guess at Soviet *intentions*, and on this basis judge whether the Ashida proposal was realistic and reasonable.

The Soviets, unlike the United States, did not demobilize their forces in the aftermath of World War II. During 1946 and 1947, Soviet ground and air units were stationed close to Japan, in an arc extending from the southernmost Kuriles and Sakhalin, down the coast of the Maritime Provinces into North Korea.[35] When they invaded the Kuriles in August,

---

35. Not surprisingly, the size and the disposition of Soviet forces in the Far East in 1946–47 do not seem to be available in any published source. This point was, however, discussed in the interviews with Mr. Suzuki and with Mr. Nishimura. Both stated that the Japanese Government had no military intelligence of its own and was not privy to U.S. or SCAP intelligence. The Government's estimate of Soviet strength in the Far East was based on its knowledge of the build-up of ground, air, and naval forces in the Maritime Provinces during 1945, in preparation for the Soviet invasion of Manchuria, Korea, southern Sakhalin, and the Kuriles. From what Japanese officials were able to gather in bits and pieces from their contacts with U.S. Occupation officials, it seemed to them that the Soviet Far Eastern forces were at least as powerful in 1947 as they had been at the end of the war in 1945.

1945, the Soviets captured four islands right off the coast of northern Hokkaido—Kunashiri, Shikotan, Etorofu, and Habomai—over which they had no previous claim, historical or otherwise. The islands are large enough for staging military operations. Habomai is less than five miles from Hokkaido; Kunashiri, only twenty miles. The southern tip of Sakhalin is only fifty miles from Hokkaido. Soviet air forces operating from these islands and from the Maritime Provinces could give direct support to an invasion force, and were also within striking distance of Japan's major industrial cities. Based on their estimate of the size and equipment of the Soviet forces stationed along this arc in 1947, the Yoshida and Katayama Governments did not think that an invasion was imminent.[36] If, however, the United States and Japan were to conclude a peace treaty without the Soviet Union, and the Occupation forces were to be withdrawn, the Soviets were thought to be in an excellent position either to threaten an attack for the purpose of exerting political pressure on a weak, unarmed Japan or actually to invade from the north.[37]

Moreover, there is evidence that when Japan surrendered in August, 1945, the Soviets hoped to occupy Hokkaido. At that time, the United States Government was willing to have Russian troops participate in the Occupation, but only if they were under General MacArthur, the Supreme Commander for the Allied Powers, as were the British and Australian units in Japan. The Soviets refused to place their units under SCAP.[38] On August 10, 1945, the Soviet Government approached United States Ambassador W. Averell Harriman in Moscow and suggested instead the creation of a joint Allied occupation force for Japan, similar to that in Germany. They proposed that a Soviet general be appointed co-commander in chief in Tokyo, with rank equal to General MacArthur's, and

36. Interviews with Suzuki and Nishimura.
37. *Ibid.*
38. Harry S. Truman, *Memoirs*, Vol. I: *Year of Decisions* (Garden City: Doubleday and Company, 1955), pp. 430–32.

that a Soviet occupation zone be established in Hokkaido. Ambassador Harriman firmly declined this proposal and notified President Truman, who approved his action.[39]

Following the exchange, Premier Stalin in a personal and secret message, dated August 16, 1945, carried the question directly to President Truman. In this message, Premier Stalin proposed that Hokkaido should be divided into northern and southern sectors by a "line running from Kushiro on the east coast of the island to the town of Rumoe on the west coast of the island"; that the surrender of Japanese forces in the northern sector should be accepted by the Soviets, rather than by General MacArthur; and that Soviet troops should occupy this sector.[40] Premier Stalin gave no indication in this message, or in other messages on this subject, that the Soviet occupation forces would accept SCAP's authority.[41] It appeared to President Truman that "Stalin was trying to bring to Japan the same kind of divided rule which the circumstances and necessities of the military situation had forced upon us in Germany."[42] He rejected Premier Stalin's proposal for a partitioned Hokkaido.[43]

The Soviets, however, persisted. Lieutenant General Kuzmo Derevyanko was sent to Tokyo as the Soviet representative to SCAP. During the fall of 1945 he continued to insist that a Soviet occupation zone be established in Hokkaido. At one point he told General MacArthur that Soviet troops would move into Hokkaido, with or without the Supreme Commander's permission.[44]

The Japanese Government got wind of these Soviet de-

---

39. *Ibid.* See also Van Aduard, p. 17.
40. The text of this message is reproduced, in exactly the same words, in Truman, I, 440, and in Ministry of Foreign Affairs of the USSR (MFAUSSR), *Stalin's Correspondence with Roosevelt and Truman, 1941–1945* (New York: Capricorn Books, 1965), p. 226.
41. MFAUSSR, pp. 267, 268.
42. Truman, I, 443.
43. The text of Truman's reply to Stalin is reproduced in Truman, I, 441, and MFAUSSR, p. 267.
44. MacArthur, p. 285.

mands.[45] From their point of view, the Soviet forces on Kunashiri, Shikotan, Etorofu, and Habomai were already in illegal occupation of Japanese territory. The threat to the main islands, especially to Hokkaido, was not to be taken lightly. Although Mr. Yoshida and Mr. Ashida did not believe in 1947 that the Soviets were about to attack Japan, it must not be forgotten that Japan was demilitarized, physically and psychologically. For the foreseeable future, the Japanese Government, unaided, would not have the means to repel even a small, lightly supported thrust into Hokkaido. Foreign Minister Ashida's proposal for a United States guarantee and for the maintenance of bases in Japan for use by the United States in an emergency was intended to deter such a thrust. In short, he believed that the Soviets would not rashly bomb a Japanese city, or land a regiment or two in Hokkaido, if doing so meant risking war with the United States. The Americans were clearly stronger in the air and on the sea. The Soviets, if intent on attacking Japan, would be more likely to make careful and massive preparations, which would give the United States and Japan time to prepare a defense.[46]

VI

THE EXTERNAL Soviet military threat was related to the internal Communist threat. The Japanese Government's anxiety over the Soviet Union's intentions was not based solely on the presence of Soviet forces in the northern islands, nor on the Soviet demands for an occupation zone in Hokkaido. When the Russians, in violation of their neutrality pact with Japan, invaded Manchuria in the closing days of the war, they made prisoners of 594,000 Japanese soldiers and civilians.[47] Following the surrender, these prisoners, unlike those

45. Interviews with Suzuki and Nishimura.
46. Interview with Suzuki.
47. From a Moscow broadcast of May 20, 1949, quoted in *Akahata*, May 22, 1949, in Roger Swearingen and Paul F. Langer, *Red Flag in Japan*

taken by the other Allied forces, were not promptly repatriated to Japan. In 1946, at American insistence, the Soviets reluctantly agreed to repatriation, on the condition that the United States provide the shipping.[48]

After many delays, the first group of prisoners finally reached Japan in the spring of 1947, and it immediately became apparent why the Soviets had moved so slowly.

The prisoners had been subjected to a thorough and intensive Communist indoctrination, which stressed that Japan was ruled and exploited by a capitalist government and was a pawn in the hands of aggressive American capitalism, which threatened the peace of the Far East and the world. They had been taught that the only recourse of the Japanese masses was to support the Japanese Communist Party (JCP).[49]

The treatment of these prisoners and their behavior upon arriving home did not suggest to the Japanese Government that the Soviets were trying to be a friendly, peaceful neighbor.[50] On the contrary, it appeared that they were intent on swinging Japan into the Soviet orbit, if not by direct attack, then by an internal Communist take-over.

This impression was strengthened by General Derevyanko's speeches before the public meetings of the Allied Council for

---

(Cambridge, Mass.: Harvard University Press, 1952), p. 232. U.S. and Japanese sources generally agree on the number of prisoners, but this is one of the few Soviet statements of the number of prisoners involved. The prisoner of war issue is treated in some detail in William J. Sebald, *With MacArthur in Japan* (New York: W. W. Norton and Company, 1965), pp. 136–48. Ambassador Sebald became diplomatic adviser to SCAP following Ambassador Atcheson's death in a plane crash in August, 1947, and he acted as U.S. representative on the Allied Council for Japan, which was the principal channel for dealing with the prisoner of war issue.

48. Sebald, pp. 136–48.
49. Swearingen and Langer, pp. 233, 234.
50. Charles A. Willoughby and John Chamberlain, *MacArthur: 1941–1945* (New York: McGraw-Hill Book Company, 1954), pp. 320–21. General Willoughby was General MacArthur's G-2 (Intelligence). General Willoughby points out that the overwhelming majority of the repatriates shed their indoctrination after a few months in Japan. In 1947, however, the repatriates looked very much like a potential Soviet fifth column. Mr. Suzuki also recalled the concern caused in official Japanese circles by the indoctrination and behavior of the repatriates.

Japan, which were followed with care by Japanese officials and newsmen. During the winter of 1946–47, General Derevyanko began criticizing SCAP in blistering language for protecting, behind a façade of parliamentarianism, certain undemocratic, reactionary Japanese—read Yoshida Government.[51] He exhorted the Japanese labor movement and the Japanese Communist Party to exercise fully their democratic rights, which, he argued, included their right to control the economy in order that the workers themselves might enjoy the fruits of their labor. Moreover, the activities of the oversized, 400-man Soviet mission in Tokyo gave substance to General Derevyanko's revolutionary speeches. For the members of the mission were attempting to assist in the organization of the newly formed Japanese labor unions.[52]

The repatriation issue, General Derevyanko's attacks on the legitimacy of the Yoshida Cabinet, and the activities of his oversized mission led the Japanese Government to fear that the labor movement would fall under the control of the Japanese Communist Party, which, in turn, would serve the ends of Soviet foreign policy.[53]

The event that more than any other crystallized the suspicions and fears of the Japanese Government over internal security was the nationwide general strike scheduled for February 1, 1947, by the left-wing Socialist and Communist leaders of the Government Workers Unions. The general strike was forbidden by SCAP and did not take place. Nevertheless, it was a dramatic demonstration of the capability and intentions of the left-wing Socialists and Communists who at that time exercised a great influence over the Occupation-sponsored labor movement. The Yoshida Government, with no police forces or military units at its disposal, believed that it

51. *Akahata*, December 16, 23, 1946. Sebald, pp. 131–34, 145.
52. Sebald, p. 134. Yoshida, *Memoirs*, pp. 213, 214. Willoughby and Chamberlain, p. 325.
53. Yoshida, *Memoirs*, pp. 226, 231–35.

was saved from insurrection and a possible Communist take-over only by SCAP's intervention.

The economic conditions behind the strike have already been outlined in the discussion of General MacArthur's peace treaty initiative. The Japanese people, especially those living in the bombed-out cities, were hungry, poorly clothed, and inade-quately housed. The inflation was wiping out their savings, rapidly diminishing their purchasing power, and threatening to sweep away the last vestiges of stability. Defeat and the Occupation reforms had already weakened their faith in authority and in the previously established order of society. Despite the good intentions of the American Occupation authorities, the future looked terribly uncertain and bleak.[54] The immediate postwar environment was ideal for the growth of a revolutionary movement, and the Japanese Communists were the best-organized revolutionaries in the country.

The fifteen-month period from October, 1945, to February, 1947, was probably the most promising and hopeful in the history of the Japanese Communist Party. From its establish-ment in 1921 until the surrender in 1945, the party had been illegal and had been harried continuously by the police, so that at any given time most of its leaders were either in prison or in exile. On October 4, 1945, however, SCAP ordered the Japanese Government immediately to abrogate or suspend all laws restricting political freedoms. The Communists were discharged from prison and returned from abroad. They hailed the Occupation forces as liberators and announced that they would assist in the demilitarization and democratization of Japan.[55]

The leading strategist of the resurgent party was Nozaka Sanzō, who spent the war years in Yenan with the Chinese Communists. Until 1950, he did his best to lead a "lovable

54. For a vivid description of the feel and tone of Japan in the early post-surrender period, see Reischauer, pp. 205–83.
55. Swearingen and Langer, pp. 87, 88. See also Yoshida, *Memoirs*, p. 227.

Communist Party" in a "peaceful revolution." In essence, Nozaka's strategy was to bring the party to power by winning leadership in the newly organized labor movement being nurtured by SCAP, and to take office in a Socialist-Communist coalition cabinet which would be based on the labor movement.[56]

During 1946 the Communists successfully penetrated the labor movement and cooperated with the left-wing Socialists. They worked their way to leadership in the key Government Workers Unions, particularly in the transportation, communications, and electric power industries.[57] The next steps in their planned drive for power were to establish a united front with the Socialists and then to "overthrow"[58] the Yoshida Cabinet. The tactics chosen were further to aggravate Japan's economic ills, saddle the ruling Conservatives with responsibility for the resulting chaos and misery, and promise to lead Japan to a socialist utopia. Conditions were seemingly ideal. SCAP was

56. Nozaka Sanzō, *Senryaku, Senjutsu no Shomondai* [Problems of Strategy and Tactics] (Tokyo: Obei Shobo, 1948), pp. 11, 74. Nihon Kyōsantō, *Nihon Kyōsantō no Susumu Michi* [The Path of Progress for the Japanese Communist Party] (Tokyo: Nihon Kyōsantō Shuppan Bu, 1949), pp. 6–8. Swearingen and Langer, pp. 134–41. Although the labor movement was the key element in the party's strategy and is most relevant to security policy, the Communists also made efforts to organize and control the farmers and the intellectuals.

57. Swearingen and Langer, pp. 155, 156. See also Shinobu, pp. 402–4, and Willoughby and Chamberlain, p. 324. As early as November, 1945, Yoshio Shiga, member of the party's Central Committee, was quoted in the party's organ as having said that the communication, transportation, and electric power industries were "the nerves of the nation." *Akahata*, November 22, 1945. Moreover, according to SCAP sources, the Communist leader Satomi Hakamada, also a member of the Central Committee, told SCAP officials in November, 1946, that "a handful of Communist Party members hold the actual leadership in these unions" (in the above industries). Supreme Commander for the Allied Powers, *Summation of Non-Military Activities in Japan,* February, 1947, p. 36.

58. The word *overthrow* or *bring down* (gakai) was used in 1947 and is still used by the left-wing Opposition to denote both a peaceful, legitimate assumption of governmental power and a violent, unconstitutional seizure of power. The moderate Socialists use it in the former sense. The radical Socialists and the Communists use it in both senses. It is an excellent word for making revolutionary-sounding speeches and for papering over differences among the left-wing Opposition, but it also leaves the governing Conservatives uncertain and uneasy over the Opposition's attachment to parliamentary institutions.

doing nothing to obstruct their efforts. Labor, suffering terribly in the inflation, naturally demanded higher and higher wages. Management was facing ruin and bankruptcy.

Throughout 1946 the tactic of economic disruption was carried out either consciously or unknowingly by the unions of the Japanese Congress of Industrial Organizations, whose members engaged in an increasing number of wildcat strikes and lockouts, and frequently took over entire plants in the name of "production control," in several cases in defiance of the Japanese police.[59]

The police, as already noted, were shorthanded and entirely under local control. Moreover, the policemen who survived the police reform were understandably intent on avoiding a confrontation with the SCAP-sponsored labor movement. In the parlance of the day, the police were "feudalistic and authoritarian," and the labor movement was "democratic and progressive." In short, the Japanese police were neither able nor willing to control labor disorders and violence.[60]

Given the state of the economy, the existing unrest, and the disorganization and weakness of the police, the Communist and Socialist policy of economic disruption, although ostensibly aimed at discrediting the Yoshida Cabinet, seemed to be leading to complete economic and social chaos, and possibly to revolutionary violence. In fact, Nozaka's opponents in the Communist Party, and among the left-wing Socialists as well, criticized him for being too timid and for not boldly exploiting this revolutionary potential.[61] The radical left, after years of persecution and prison, tingled at the possibilities. And in the background was General Derevyanko, making inflamma-

59. Swearingen and Langer, p. 155. Yoshida, *Memoirs,* pp. 78–84. Shinobu, pp. 360–79, 395–418.
60. Yoshida, *Memoirs,* pp. 176–81. Interviews with Suzuki and Nishimura. Kennan, *Memoirs,* p. 390. Mr. Kennan, as director of the Policy Planning Staff, became deeply concerned over Japan's vulnerability to an internal Communist take-over in the fall of 1947; he visited Japan in February, 1948, to get a firsthand view of the situation and to discuss it with General MacArthur.
61. Swearingen and Langer, pp. 222–29.

tory speeches before the Allied Council, and his busy, 400-man Soviet mission.

Prime Minister Yoshida could do nothing to fundamentally improve economic conditions. He attempted to remain in power and to maintain a semblance of peace and order by forming a national coalition government of his own Liberal Party, the Democratic Party, and the Socialist Party, hoping to draw the more moderate, right-wing Socialists into the cabinet, and thus forestall the united front and isolate the radicals. He pointed out to SCAP the dangers of permitting the Communists a free hand in the labor movement, and he publicly decried labor violence.[62] He was appalled at the weakness of the undermanned local police forces, and on several occasions urged SCAP to permit the creation of a centralized, effective national force to supplement the local units.[63] But he failed in all these efforts. SCAP did not respond to his warnings and advice. The Democratic Party was reluctant to enter the national coalition, and the Socialists demanded more cabinet posts than Mr. Yoshida was willing to concede.

Then, in January of 1947, the crisis came to a head. The Communists and left-wing Socialists, although not formally allied in a united front, seemed to be making their bid for office. The 2,600,000-man Government Workers Unions, including the Communist-led railroad, electric power, and communications unions, were pressing the Yoshida Government for a wage increase. On January 11, after much advance publicity, the union leaders announced that negotiations had failed, and called for a nationwide general strike on February 1. If carried

62. Yoshida, *Memoirs*, p. 81.
63. *Ibid.*, pp. 176–81. Mr. Kennan made similar recommendations, but without visible effect. Kennan, *Memoirs*, pp. 390–93. Shinobu, p. 505, quotes Ball, p. 106, to the effect that the Yoshida Government, early in 1947, "sounded out allied representatives on the prospects of being allowed a standing army of 100,000 men and a small air force." Mr. Ball, an Australian, was understandably prone to interpret Prime Minister Yoshida's desire for internal police forces as a first step in rearmament. Shinobu agrees with this interpretation. Events in 1951, however, were to show that Mr. Yoshida had no intention of rearming. See Chapter Three.

out, the strike would have crippled the entire economy and might have led to widespread disorders and violence. The labor leaders knew this. The Government knew this. And so did SCAP.

General MacArthur was loath to intervene openly. To do so was contrary to his basic Occupation policy of exerting indirect control in Japan; moreover, he does not appear to have been eager to deal a blow to the labor unions. As he understood his mission, he was to foster a responsible labor movement.[64] Intervention and perhaps suppression of the general strike would have been an admission of his failure to accomplish this mission. From January 11 until January 31, SCAP, through the Labor Division of its Economic and Scientific Section, attempted to persuade the union leaders to call off the general strike. General William F. Marquat, chief of the Economic and Scientific Section, and Theodore Cohen, of the Labor Division, told the strike leaders that the Government would meet most of their demands for a wage increase, and that SCAP was planning general elections for the coming spring, which the leftist parties had a good chance of winning.[65] The union leaders wavered and argued among themselves, but were unwilling or unable to call off the scheduled general strike. Finally, at 2:30 on the afternoon before the strike was to begin, General MacArthur prohibited the strike in a nationwide radio broadcast.[66]

Although no official mention was made of them, the 78,000 troops of the United States Occupation forces stood ready to enforce SCAP's prohibition. Later in the afternoon, the Communist Party issued a call to the Government Workers Unions to assert their democratic right to strike in defiance of General MacArthur. The Communist call went unheeded. There was no general strike. Less than a week later, however,

64. MacArthur, pp. 308–10.
65. Shinobu, pp. 474, 475.
66. For text of broadcast, see MacArthur, pp. 308, 309.

on February 6, General MacArthur sent Prime Minister Yoshida a letter urging that general elections be called as soon as practicable.[67]

The evidence is not conclusive, but it appears that SCAP avoided the general strike by the threat of suppression, combined with the promise of elections and, finally, General Mac-Arthur's public prohibition, which saved the union leaders from having to cancel the strike themselves, a move which would have implied that they had made a bargain with SCAP. All the while, the Yoshida Cabinet stood by helplessly, unable either to protect itself or to bargain for its own future.

The abortive general strike did leave SCAP disenchanted with the Communists, but at the time there was little indication that future elected Governments would fare better than the first Yoshida Cabinet. General MacArthur's letter of February 6 left Prime Minister Yoshida with no choice but to call for elections under circumstances that were almost certain to mean defeat. SCAP showed no sign of permitting the Japanese Government to build a police force which would enable it to protect itself against future intimidation by the labor movement. The Communists and left-wing Socialists seemed to have been rewarded for their policy of economic disruption, and they were left free to practice it in the future. In fact, to the surprise of Mr. Yoshida and the chagrin of SCAP and the moderate Socialists, the Government Workers Unions refused to cooperate with Prime Minister Katayama's Socialist-led administration, and proved a serious obstacle to the implementation of the Prime Minister's economic policy.[68]

When the Japanese Government, in the Ashida memorandum, stated that it would itself "suppress any internal riots and disorders," and that it wished to "build up its domestic

67. For text of letter, see SCAP, *Political Reorientation of Japan,* II, 521. See also Yoshida, *Memoirs,* p. 82.
68. Yoshida, *Memoirs,* p. 215. See also Swearingen and Langer, pp. 157–59.

police forces, on the ground and on the sea," it had the planned general strike of February 1 freshly in mind. Although Foreign Minister Ashida had himself won office partly as a result of that abortive strike, he realized what a dangerous precedent had been set.[69] Future labor disorders and general strikes were probable, and the Communists and radical Socialists could be expected to encourage and exploit them in an effort to come to power. Following the conclusion of a peace treaty and the withdrawal of the Occupation forces, the Japanese Government would need an effective, centrally controlled police force if it were to prevent a Communist take-over. This was the internal threat to Japan's security, and the means proposed by the Japanese Government to counter it. On balance, the danger of an internal Communist take-over appeared at least comparable to, and probably greater than, the danger of a direct Soviet attack.[70]

VII

IT WOULD BE a mistake to conclude from the Ashida memorandum that the Japanese Government was exaggerating the Communist threat, or that the Japanese were attempting to exploit this threat in order to persuade the United States Government to make a separate peace. Mr. Yoshida and Mr. Ashida considered a United States–Soviet split to be likely, but they were under no illusions that they could precipitate it.[71] They did, however, want the United States Government to know that, if a split occurred, they would be willing to conclude a separate peace and to cooperate with the United States

69. Interview with Suzuki.

70. Interestingly, Mr. Kennan held this view. He did not think that the Soviets would intervene with their military forces in Japan until the process of subversion was well advanced. He believed that the key to Japan's defense was internal security, which required economic recovery and stability and the building of adequate internal security forces, including maritime forces to prevent infiltration along Japan's sea coast. Kennan, *Memoirs,* pp. 387–93. Mr. Yoshida's views were very similar. See *Memoirs,* pp. 82, 212–14.

71. Interviews with Suzuki and Nishimura.

in preventing a Communist take-over of Japan, either by a Soviet invasion or by a Communist-led insurrection. Although the Japanese Government believed that both the internal and external threats were real, and was planning countermeasures, it was not calling for an ideological crusade backed by huge military forces to turn back the Red tide. The Government was not even proposing that Japan be permitted to rebuid its armed forces. On the contrary, in the Ashida memorandum the Japanese Government took the position that Japan would be adequately defended against direct Soviet attack by a United States guarantee, by the presence of United States forces in the areas adjacent to Japan, and by the maintenance in Japan of bases which the United States could use in an emergency. The Japanese Government would handle the threat of an internal Communist take-over by building national paramilitary police forces.

Although more than two decades have passed since the Ashida memorandum was composed, the circumstances which led to its preparation and the ideas it embodied are still highly relevant to an understanding of Japanese defense policy. Since 1948, Japan has been ruled by a succession of Conservative prime ministers and cabinets whose views on national security were largely shaped by the events described above. With the partial exception of Prime Minister Hato-yama [72] (December, 1954, to December, 1956) these men have all acted in accordance with the basic assumptions and policy proposals in the Ashida memorandum. Prime Ministers Yoshida, Hatoyama, Kishi, Ikeda, and Sato have made defense policy in the belief that the Soviet Union has posed the principal if not the only, external threat to Japan; [73] and

72. See pp. 76–79 (Prime Minister Hatoyama's defense policy.)
73. For a discussion of the Sato Government's strategic estimates, see ch. 6. The available evidence indicates that the Sato Government has continued to see the Soviet Union as the chief external military threat to Japan, despite the gradual improvement in Soviet-Japanese political and economic relations. Although recognizing that Communist China may become dangerous in the future, the Government has not considered China as an immediate, serious

that internally it has been necessary to guard against a Communist take-over which would be staged against a background of labor disorders and violence. Under these men the Government has consistently sought to provide for Japan's security by means of (1) a mutual defense agreement with the United States which would include a guarantee against direct attack and (2) Japanese forces capable of maintaining internal security. Compromises were necessary, but these basic policy goals were to shape the Japanese Government's approach to the 1951 and 1960 Security Treaties, and also to the building of the Self-Defense Forces.

---

external threat. The Government has taken the position that China's limited nuclear capability is more than offset by the American nuclear umbrella, and that China's conventional naval and air forces are not powerful enough to endanger the Japanese islands or Japanese shipping. It is believed, however, that the Peking Government is a source of encouragement and support for a "war of national liberation" in Japan, and is therefore a limited threat to Japan's internal security.

The Soviets, on the other hand, not only are a nuclear superpower but have also been increasing their naval and air capability, and are believed to be more mobile and better equipped for limited, conventional war in East Asia than at any time since the end of World War II. Thus, it appears that the Sato Government has been suspicious of both Communist Chinese and Soviet intentions, and has based its estimate of the threats posed by Communist China and the Soviet Union on their military capabilities.

THREE

፭ጌ፭ጌ፭ጌ፭ጌ፭ጌ፭ጌ፭ጌ

Defense Policy and the 1951
Security Treaty

I

ON THE RELATIONSHIP between the Ashida memorandum
and the United States–Japanese Security Treaty of 1951, Mr.
Yoshida wrote:

Although it [the Ashida memorandum] did not positively express
a desire for the stationing of United States forces in Japan, I think
it is fair to say that its underlying trend of thought was identical
with the basic conception of the United States–Japan security
system.

I formed my second cabinet in October, 1948, but since my ideas
on security policy did not differ from those of the Katayama Cabinet, I saw no necessity despite the change in cabinets to alter
their policy. Although there may have been changes in detail, there
were no substantive developments on the issue until Special Ambassador Dulles came to Japan in January, 1951.[1]

Mr. Yoshida's remarks were directed, in part, to the Socialists and the Democrats, who bitterly opposed the 1951 Security Treaty. He was saying in effect that in 1947 Foreign
Minister Ashida had proposed and Prime Minister Katayama
had approved the underlying conception of the treaty, and
that their later criticisms flowed not from a sincere differ-
ence over policy but rather from the fact that they were not
in power when the treaty was made.

Although intended in part for domestic political consumption, this statement does, nevertheless, establish a link between

1. Yoshida, *Kaisō Jūnen*, II, 114.

the 1947 memorandum and the policy implemented in 1951, and at the same time it raises several vital questions on the nature of that link. To what extent were the 1947 proposals embodied in the 1951 treaty? Is there any evidence that Prime Minister Yoshida actually attempted to realize the policy set forth in the Ashida memorandum when he negotiated the 1951 treaty? And lastly, what were the "substantive developments" which occurred when Special Ambassador John Foster Dulles came to Japan in January, 1951?

In the Ashida memorandum it was proposed that, after concluding peace, Japan be protected against a Communist take-over by means of a mutual defense agreement with the United States, under which the United States would guarantee Japan against a direct Soviet attack and would station certain of its forces in the areas adjacent to Japan, probably on Okinawa and the Bonins. Japan would agree to the maintenance of bases in the country for emergency use by the United States, and the Japanese Government would build national police forces capable of preventing an internal Communist take-over.

On the face of it, the 1951 Security Treaty bears little resemblance to the Ashida memorandum. The treaty was not a mutual defense agreement. There were no provisions for joint consultation or joint action.[2] Japan granted and the United States accepted the right to continue to station its armed forces in Japan.[3] The United States did not explicitly guarantee Japan against external attack. It only stated, in the preamble to the treaty, that it was "*willing* to maintain certain of its armed forces in and about Japan,"[4] and in Article I that:

---

2. "Security Treaty Between Japan and the United States of America," U.S. Department of State, *United States Treaties and Other International Agreements*, pp. 3329–32.
    3. *Ibid.*, Article I.
    4. *Ibid.*, Preamble. Italics added.

Such forces *may* be utilized to contribute to the maintenance of international peace and security in the Far East and to the security of Japan against armed attack from without, including assistance given at the express request of the Japanese Government to put down large-scale internal riots and disturbances in Japan, caused through instigation or intervention by an outside power or powers.[5]

Thus, to the extent that the United States was obligated to protect Japan at all, its obligation applied to both external and internal security. The Ashida memorandum had proposed that the Japanese Government take full responsibility for internal security. It is, however, important to note that the 1951 treaty was a "provisional arrangement," [6] intended to provide Japan temporarily with a measure of security "in the expectation . . . that Japan will itself increasingly assume responsibility for its own defense against direct and indirect aggression." [7] Finally, the treaty would only be terminated when both governments agreed that it was no longer necessary.[8] This was an unusual provision which meant that the United States was obligated to keep its troops in Japan as long as the Japanese Government wanted them; but also that the Japanese Government was obligated to have United States forces in Japan as long as the United States wanted to keep them there.

The only proposal of the Ashida memorandum embodied in these security arrangements was the United States guarantee, and this guarantee was realized not so much in the vague language of the treaty as in the actual presence of United States forces in Japan. It was inconceivable that the Soviet Union could attack Japan while United States forces were stationed there without evoking an American military re-

5. *Ibid.*, Article I. In the Japanese text the phrase translated as "may be utilized" is "shiyo suru koto ga dekiru." Italics added.
6. *Ibid.*, Preamble.
7. *Ibid.*
8. *Ibid.*, Article IV.

sponse. This *de facto* guarantee is not to be sniffed at. Of the two basic goals of the Ashida memorandum—the United States guarantee and the mutual agreement—the guarantee was probably the more essential. It is well to remember that in 1951 Japan was still extremely weak economically and militarily. The two continental giants, the Soviet Union and Communist China, had recently formed a military alliance and were actively cooperating in the Korean War in an apparent effort to gain control over the entire peninsula. Japan was in no position to defend itself. It needed outside help, with or without benefit of mutuality.

But why was Prime Minister Yoshida not successful in writing provisions for joint consultation and action into the treaty? Why did he fail to obtain an explicit American guarantee against direct attack? And why did the treaty provide for the possibility of United States intervention to maintain internal security?

II

THE ANSWERS to these questions lie in the differences between the United States and Japanese Governments that came to light in the course of the security treaty negotiations between Prime Minister Yoshida and Ambassador Dulles. In April, 1950, President Truman appointed Mr. Dulles as a foreign policy adviser to the Secretary of State, to take charge of the Japanese peace settlement and post-peace treaty security arrangements. The appointment was indicative of the dramatic changes in the international situation and in American Far Eastern policy which had occurred since 1947, when the Ashida memorandum had failed to evoke a response in Washington. The United States–Soviet split anticipated by Mr. Yoshida and Mr. Ashida had become the cold war. The civil strife in China had halted in the fall of 1949, with the Communists in control of the mainland and the Nationalists on Taiwan. In February of 1950, the Chinese Communist Government concluded with the Soviet Union a Treaty of Friendship, Alliance, and Mutual Assistance which was directed specifically against Japan.[9]

On the other hand, although Soviet power seemed to be greatly augmented by the victory of the Chinese Communists and the conclusion of the Sino-Soviet alliance, its policy in Korea suggested that the Soviet Union might be willing to settle for a secure defensive position in Northeast Asia, one that would not threaten Japan militarily. The United States Government, for its part, seemed willing tacitly to accept such an arrangement. During 1948 and 1949, the Soviets and the Americans had withdrawn most of their troops from Korea, leaving behind a pro-Soviet Government north of the 38th parallel, and a pro-American Government in the south.[10] And in January, 1950, the United States Government let it be known that it was planning to form a Far Eastern defense perimeter stretching from the Aleutian Islands, through Japan and Okinawa south to the Philippines.[11] The future of Taiwan

9. "Treaty of Friendship, Alliance and Mutual Assistance Between the Union of Soviet Socialist Republics and the People's Republic of China (February 14, 1950)," in United Nations, Secretariat, *United Nations Treaty Series*, X, 334–38. According to Article I, "Both High Contracting Parties undertake jointly to take all the necessary measures at their disposal for the purpose of preventing a repetition of aggression and violation of peace on the part of Japan or any other state which should unite with Japan, directly or indirectly, in acts of aggression."

10. Relatively fair and well-documented accounts of Soviet and United States policy in Korea during 1948–50 can be found in Max Beloff, *Soviet Policy in the Far East, 1944–1951* (London: Oxford University Press, 1953); in Coral Bell, "Korea and the Balance of Power," *The Political Quarterly*, XXV (January–March, 1954), 17–29; and in Wilbur H. Hitchcock, "North Korea Jumps the Gun," *Current History*, XX, No. 115 (March, 1951), 136–44. Two important participatory accounts are Truman, Vol. II: *Years of Trial and Hope*, pp. 317–31; and Kennan, *Memoirs*, pp. 394–96.

11. Secretary of State Dean Acheson's highly controversial address to the National Press Club on January 12, 1950. For text, see Council on Foreign Relations, *The United States in World Affairs, 1950*, ed. R. P. Stebbins (New York: Harper and Row, 1951), p. 200. Also, General MacArthur, in his interview with the *Daily Mail* (London) correspondent, G. Ward Price, on March 2, 1949, stated: "It [the U.S. Asian defense line] starts from the Philippines and continues through the Ryukyu Archipelago which includes its main bastion Okinawa. Then it bends back through Japan and the Aleutian chain to Alaska." *The Mainichi*, March 3, 1949.

was unclear. But following the mutual withdrawal of Soviet and American forces from Korea, it appeared that the peninsula might become a buffer zone, enhancing the security of Japan, as well as that of the Soviet Union and Communist China.

In brief, it was known in Tokyo that the United States wanted to stabilize the Far East by means of a Western Pacific defense perimeter which would include Japan and a Korean buffer zone, and that in order to implement this policy the Truman Administration intended to conclude peace with Japan without Soviet participation, if necessary, and to make a security treaty with Japan.[12] Washington had been edging in this direction for several years, but the appointment of Mr. Dulles to take charge of all the negotiations attendant on the peace and security treaties indicated to Prime Minister Yoshida that the Americans meant business.[13] Apart from his reputation as a capable and forceful diplomatist, Mr. Dulles had the added qualification of being a prominent Republican. The Republicans in the Senate, who were numerous enough to block ratification, were not likely to obstruct the handiwork of their shadow Secretary of State.

Prime Minister Yoshida had also learned that the United States Government wanted to continue to station its forces in Japan after concluding the peace treaty, but it was not clear what the function and size of those forces would be. For domestic political reasons, Mr. Yoshida wanted a sharp reduction, if not a complete withdrawal, of the United States forces.[14]

12. Yoshida, *Kaisō Jūnen*, II, 118, 119. Also interview with Mr. Nishimura, who in his position as chief of the Foreign Ministry Treaty Bureau was in close touch with Mr. Yoshida during this period and accompanied him to most of the high level meetings and discussions in preparation for the peace settlement.

13. Yoshida, *Memoirs*, p. 249.

14. Nishimura Kumao, "Nichi Bei Anzen Hoshō Jōyaku no Seiritsu Jijō" [Making the U.S.–Japanese Security Treaty], in Kotani Hidejirō and Tanaka Naokichi, eds., *Nihon no Anzen Hoshō* [Japan's Security] (Tokyo: Kajima Shuppan Kai, 1964), p. 205.

He hoped that he and Mr. Dulles would be able to find some middle ground on this issue.

From Prime Minister Yoshida's point of view, the distribution of power in the Far East in the spring of 1950 was similar to that anticipated when the Ashida memorandum had been prepared in 1947, and it still provided a workable basis for Japan's defense policy. He did not believe that the Communist victory in China added much to the threat of external attack. China had neither air nor naval forces capable of reaching Japan, and given the devastated condition of China's economy and the meagerness of its industry, it would be years before it could hope to produce such forces. The Soviet threat from the north was still the primary external threat, and it still seemed to Prime Minister Yoshida that an American guarantee, American forces around Japan, and emergency-use bases in the country would neutralize the Soviet threat. The prospect of a Korean buffer zone added to the feasibility of this arrangement.[15]

Within Japan, although there were distinct signs of economic recovery and stability, the labor movement was still in ferment and led by radicals, and the Japanese Communist Party, under instructions from Moscow, had discarded Nozaka Sanzō's "peaceful revolution" in favor of a more violent, openly insurrectionary line.[16] The previous summer had been marred by crippling strikes and labor violence, which had led Prime Minister Yoshida once again unsuccessfully to urge SCAP to permit the establishment of national police forces for the maintenance of internal security.[17]

In June, 1950, ambassador Dulles flew to Tokyo to discuss his assignment with General MacArthur and to sound out Japanese opinion on the peace settlement. Prime Minister Yoshida and his colleagues wanted in turn to sound out American policy

15. Interview with Nishimura.
16. Swearingen and Langer, p. 222.
17. Yoshida, *Memoirs*, pp. 179–80.

on Japan's future security as it related to the peace settlement. Mr. Dulles caught them off balance by seeking only general agreement on the necessity for resisting Communist aggression, and then strongly urging that Japan begin to rearm. Mr. Yoshida, still struggling with SCAP for a national police force, was unprepared for Mr. Dulles' ideas on rearmament.[18] Neither side found the meetings productive.[19] But perhaps it was just as well that nothing definite was settled upon. For before Mr. Dulles left Japan, events in Korea radically changed the assumptions on which both Governments were operating.

III

ON JUNE 25, North Korean armies unexpectedly invaded South Korea. President Truman responded by dispatching the United States forces in Japan to Korea, under United Nations auspices. Suddenly, the Korean buffer zone was gone, and within a few months there would not be sufficient American troops in Japan to maintain civil order, if it should become necessary again to do so. Prime Minister Yoshida believed that it was an axiom of Japanese foreign policy that South Korea must not be permitted to fall into the hands of a hostile power.[20] And as might be expected, the rapid reduction of

18. Interview with Nishimura. See also Yoshida, *Memoirs*, p. 265. In his own account, Mr. Yoshida makes no mention of his reaction to Mr. Dulles' rearmament proposal. In Ambassador William J. Sebald's account of this meeting, at which he was present, the Ambassador writes: "Dulles, a man not given to small talk under any circumstances, tried to steer the conversation toward a discussion of Japan's security. Yoshida would have none of this. Smiling and with chuckles, he spoke with circumlocutory indirectness, with vagueness, and with an astute use of parables. He refused to commit himself in the slightest way. 'Yes,' he said, 'security for Japan is possible, and the United States can take care of it. But Japan's amour propre must be preserved in doing so.' " Sebald, p. 257.

19. Sebald, p. 257. Dunn, p. 104

20. For reasons that will be discussed later in this chapter, Prime Minister Yoshida and his successors have avoided stating this proposition publicly. Mr. Nishimura, however, stated that Prime Minister Yoshida held strongly to this view of Korea and considered it a basic principle of Japan's foreign and defense policy, comparable in certain respects to the British axiom that the Lowlands must not be permitted to fall into hostile hands.

American forces in Japan left him concerned over internal security.[21] General MacArthur quickly changed his stand on the police question, however, and within a few weeks of the outbreak of the war he authorized the formation of a 75,000-man National Police Reserve force, which would be equipped by the United States. Prime Minister Yoshida was doubly relieved by this decision. It promised a solution to the internal security problem, and he hoped it would satisfy Ambassador Dulles' request for rearmament.[22]

As for the war in Korea, neither Prime Minister Yoshida nor General MacArthur seem to have believed that Japan could or should have sent troops to fight there.[23] For even if the Japanese had been willing and able to do so, they knew that the South Koreans would never have permitted a Japanese expeditionary force to land.[24] Consequently, it was understood in the Japanese Government that the sixteen-nation United Nations Unified Command, led by the United States, would fight to protect Japan's security interest in Korea.

In order to fight in Korea, however, the Unified Command, staffed principally by Americans, would require an extensive network of support and logistical bases in Japan. American and other United Nations forces would pass through Japan

21. Yoshida, *Memoirs*, p. 180.
22. Interview with Nishimura.
23. MacArthur, p. 331. See also Robert D. Murphy, *Diplomat among Warriors* (Garden City: Doubleday and Company, 1964), pp. 346–49.
24. The degree of animosity between the South Korean and Japanese Governments during the Korean War is vividly described in Murphy, pp. 346, 348. As United States ambassador to Japan in 1952–53, Mr. Murphy attempted, without success, to improve relations between the two countries, and to promote cooperation in the war effort. Although it was top-secret information at the time, a sizable group of Japanese shipping and railroad men did serve in Korea under American and United Nations commands. These men were experts on Korean harbor and transportation facilities, which they had built and run while Korea was a Japanese colony. Mr. Murphy opines that "the Allied forces would have had difficulty remaining in Korea without this assistance from thousands of Japanese specialists who were familiar with that country." Yet, as he points out, animosity toward Japan was so great in South Korea that even these Japanese civilians, performing an inconspicuous but vital role in South Korea's defense, were made to feel thoroughly unwelcome. In fact, President Syngman Rhee did his best to have them sent home, and on several occasions tried to have them all arrested.

en route to Korea, would train in Japan, be supplied from depots in Japan, and receive medical care in military hospitals in Japan. In fact, the United Nations Command Headquarters for Korea was located in Tokyo throughout the war, and remained there until 1957, when it was moved to Seoul.[25]

Japan's involvement and interest in the defense of South Korea was formally acknowledged by Prime Minister Yoshida in an exchange of notes with Secretary of State Dean Acheson on September 8, 1951, the day the Security Treaty was signed. In the Acheson-Yoshida notes, the United States Government, acting on behalf of the United Nations Unified Command, requested and received from the Japanese Government a formal commitment to continue "to permit and facilitate the support in and about Japan . . . of the forces engaged in . . . United Nations action" in the Far East, after the Peace and Security Treaties came into effect.[26] In short, the Japanese Government agreed that the American bases in Japan would continue to support operations in Korea, not merely for the duration of the hostilities, but for as long as there were American bases in Japan and a United Nations Command in Korea. The Acheson-Yoshida notes were renewed in 1960 and, although rarely mentioned outside government circles, are still in effect today.

IV

THUS, FOR Prime Minister Yoshida, the Korean War settled the question of whether it would be necessary to have United States forces stationed in the country after the conclusion of the peace treaty. He concluded that it would be in order to prevent South Korea from falling under Soviet control. On

---

25. "Exchange of Notes in United Nations Command (Rear)," Headquarters, United States Forces Japan, *United States–Japan Treaties, Agreements and Other Documents*, May 1, 1961. United Nations Command (Rear) for Korea is still located in Tokyo.

26. "Acheson-Yoshida Exchange of Notes Signed at San Francisco, September 8, 1951," *ibid.*, p. 20.

this basis, he resumed planning for the security treaty. During August and September, 1950, he discussed the security question with two groups of advisers: one drawn from business and financial circles, the other from former general officers of the defunct Imperial Army and Navy.[27] He laid before these men two proposals for a security treaty.[28] The first provided for a "collective" defense agreement within the framework of the United Nations Charter, for the continued stationing of United States troops in Japan, and for joint action by the United States and Japan, under Article 51 of the United Nations Charter, to repel an armed attack on Japan. The second proposal called for the disarmament and neutralization of the entire Korean peninsula and Japan, and for a security guarantee of the Western Pacific and East Asia by the United States, the United Kingdom, the Soviet Union, and China, each of which would agree to maintain certain authorized forces in the area to be designated in the treaty.

Both groups of advisers clearly favored the proposal for a collective security arrangement. Several of the former military group said that they considered the neutralization proposal dangerously unrealistic.[29] Prime Minister Yoshida assured these men that the neutralization proposal was a back-up plan, and that he would only put it forward if there were dramatic changes in Korea, or in United States Far Eastern policy, by which he probably meant an American decision to pull out of Korea, and perhaps out of Japan too. As it turned out, Prime Minister Yoshida had no need to resort to

27. Interview with Nishimura, who was present at these meetings and took notes on the proceedings.

28. *Ibid.* The proposals are mentioned in their later form as draft treaties in Nishimura Kumao, *Anzen Hoshō Jōyaku Ron* [The Security Treaty] (Tokyo: Jiji Tsushin Sha, 1959), p. 34. Kōsaka Masataka, in his "Saishō Yoshida Shigeru Ron" [Prime Minister Yoshida Shigeru], *Chūō Kōron* (February, 1965), p. 106, also makes reference to these meetings.

29. Kōsaka, "Saishō Yoshida Shigeru Ron," p. 106. Kōsaka writes that Shimomura, who was war minister in the Higashkuni Cabinet (August to October, 1945), argued that the neutralization scheme would only be practicable if the zone included parts of Russia and China, and that this appeared impossible under the existing conditions. Also, interview with Nishimura.

this back-up plan during the negotiations with Ambassador Dulles. His problems were to be of a different order.

The question of rearmament did not take much time in these discussions. It was generally agreed that for the time being, Japan was neither economically nor psychologically prepared to rearm, and that the National Police Reserve (NPR) represented the maximum contribution Japan could make to its own defense.[30] Moreover, Prime Minister Yoshida and most of his advisers believed that, before any rearmament program could be undertaken, it would be necessary to amend Article IX of the Constitution, which forbids the maintenance of "land, sea and air forces, as well as other war potential." [31] The major topic of these discussions was the stationing of American forces in Japan after the peace treaty. With very few exceptions, both groups agreed with Prime Minister Yoshida that Japan's security interest in Korea made such an arrangement unavoidable. Prime Minister Yoshida and his advisers believed that their chief problem was to gain popular approval for the continued presence of American forces in the country: firstly, because this approval was necessary for the effective operation of the treaty; secondly, because their own political futures were tied to the treaty. There were a number of references to the Weimar Republic. It was generally believed that the principal cause of the failure of the Weimar Republic was its identification with the unpopular, punitive Versailles Treaty of 1919. Prime Minister Yoshida shared the

30. This point is also made, although not with direct reference to these conferences, in Yoshida, *Memoirs*, p. 267.

31. Mr. Ashida had recently taken the position in public that rearmament for defensive purposes was not in violation of Article IX. Mr. Nishimura explained that Prime Minister Yoshida believed that this interpretation of Article IX was essentially an attempt by Mr. Ashida to convince the United States Government that it would be better served by negotiating the peace settlement with him and a Government led by the Democratic Party, rather than with Mr. Yoshida and the Liberals—a change of cabinets which he thought might be brought about by a breakdown in the treaty negotiations and by open American displeasure with Mr. Yoshida. As a result, relations between Prime Minister Yoshida and Mr. Ashida were poor throughout the negotiations. Interview with Nishimura.

concern that a punitive treaty might be imposed on Japan. He assured the advisory groups that General MacArthur was determined to make a nonpunitive peace settlement, and that he believed that on this point Ambassador Dulles and the Government in Washington were at one with SCAP.

Prime Minister Yoshida explained that his approach to this problem was to make the peace treaty, the general security arrangements, and the specific terms of the base-leasing agreement into separate documents. The peace treaty would restore Japan's sovereignty, completely intact, and the security treaty would be an exercise of that sovereignty.[32] Moreover, he was proposing to build the security treaty on the peace-loving democratic principles of the United Nations Charter, a proposal which he expected to be helpful in gaining popular approval. The advisers agreed that these were reasonable arguments and, in the circumstances, the best possible political tactics. But at the same time, all expected the opposition parties to concentrate their fire on the security treaty and to attempt to discredit the Government for continuing the American Occupation under disguise. The general prognosis among the advisers was that Prime Minister Yoshida was clever enough and tough enough to push the treaties through, but that the planned security treaty with the United States would never gain the popularity of the old Anglo-Japanese alliance. At best, it would be accepted as the unavoidable *quid pro quo* for the nonpunitive peace settlement—a concession to irresistible American pressure. As time would show, this was an accurate prognosis.

No one seems to have suggested at these meetings that continuing to station American forces in the country should be publicly justified on the grounds that it was necessary to have United States logistical and support bases in Japan in order that the United Nations could fight to protect Japan's security

32. Interview with Nishimura. Mr. Yoshida also sets forth this approach to the treaties in *Kaisō Jūnen,* II, 115–18.

in South Korea—which was, of course, the real reason. It would be permissible in defending the treaty to refer vaguely to the emergency situation created by the Korean War, but nothing more explicit was contemplated. To begin with, Prime Minister Yoshida shared with his advisers a predisposition against discussing the real elements of high policy in public. And greatly reinforcing this prejudice was the political sensitivity of Japan's interest in Korea. The axiom that Japan's security required that South Korea not be permitted to fall into the hands of a hostile power had been a keystone of pre-war foreign policy. It was associated with Japanese imperialism in Korea and with the related policy of military expansion on the Asian continent, which most Japanese believed had led Japan into the disastrous Pacific War. To invoke this axiom would have been to invoke the whole discredited policy and to have invited disaster at the polls—an invocation and an invitation which Prime Minister Yoshida and his successors have assiduously avoided.

V

IN OCTOBER, Prime Minister Yoshida instructed Mr. Nishimura Kumao, chief of the Treaty Bureau of the Foreign Ministry, to prepare draft treaties on the basis of his two proposals, for use in the negotiations with Ambassador Dulles scheduled to be held in Tokyo that winter.[33] Mr. Nishimura had been present at the preparatory discussions in August and September. He knew what Prime Minister Yoshida wanted in the draft treaties. Still, Prime Minister Yoshida and Mr. Nishimura carefully went over the main points of the collective security proposal, and when they did so, they referred to the Ashida memorandum.[34] They hoped to mollify Mr. Ashida and Mr. Katayama, and to lessen the Democratic and Socialist parties'

33. Nishimura, "Seiritsu Jijō," p. 206.
34. Interview with Nishimura.

opposition to the treaty by incorporating as much as possible of the 1947 memorandum into the draft security treaty. Mr. Yoshida had given up the proposal for emergency-use bases, but he still intended to get a guarantee for Japan's external security and a mutual agreement—two basic goals on which he thought he could gain some support from the opposition. In addition, Mr. Nishimura was given to understand that the base-leasing provisions were to be made as attractive as possible. What was needed, in the Prime Minister's words, was a "silk hat" to dress up this unattractive reality. The "silk hat" was to be cut from the material of the United Nations Charter, and specifically from the concept of collective security.[35]

In November, Mr. Nishimura had ready a draft security treaty which included the following provisions:[36]

1. Under the Charter of the United Nations and its Constitution, Japan has the right of self-defense against an unprovoked attack, and can cooperate with the United States in accordance with the Charter, to take necessary measures to repel aggression against Japan.

2. In the event that the United Nations determines that armed aggression has been committed against Japan, the United States agrees to take the military measures necessary to repel such an aggression. Japan, in the exercise of its right of self-defense, will cooperate with the United States in repelling such an aggression.

3. In the event that an armed attack is made against Japan, the United States and Japan will take necessary measures of individual and collective self-defense to repel such an attack in accordance with Article 51 of the United Nations Charter.[37]

35. *Ibid.* This point is also confirmed by the efforts to relate the treaty to the concept of collective security in Mr. Nishimura's book and article, and in *Kaisō Jūnen.*

36. Nishimura, "Seiritsu Jijō," pp. 207, 208. See also *idem, Jōyaku Ron,* pp. 28, 29. This is not a reproduction of the draft treaty but rather a list of the items dealt with in the drafts. Mr. Nishimura, in his book and article, lists only three items but mentions others on the same pages. When interviewed, Mr. Nishimura checked this translation and made a number of corrections and clarifications.

37. Item 2 provides for measures to repel aggression *after* the U.N. has determined that Japan has been attacked. Item 3 provides for measures to repel an attack on Japan *before or in lieu of* a U.N. determination that an act of aggression has taken place. Article 51 states: "Nothing in the present

4. Since Japan is unarmed, the Parties agree to the stationing of United States forces in Japan, in order to make possible the implementation of Articles 2 and 3.

5. A joint United States–Japanese committee will be formed to facilitate consultation and cooperation on matters relating to Japan's security, and on the stationing of United States forces in Japan.

6. The treaty will be made effective for a period of fifteen years.

No mention was made in the draft of Japan's internal security. The Japanese Government was in the process of organizing and training the National Police Reserve, and Prime Minister Yoshida still believed that the internal-external security equation of the Ashida memorandum had relevance to the security agreement. But he instructed Mr. Nishimura to make no reference in the draft treaty to internal security, since to do so would raise further questions on whether the peace settlement was truly restoring Japan's sovereignty—an issue which had already been sufficiently complicated by the decision to retain United States forces in Japan after concluding the peace treaty.[38]

VI

ON JANUARY 25, 1951, Mr. Dulles arrived in Japan, and negotiations were begun in earnest on the security treaty.[39]

Charter shall impair the inherent right of individual or collective self-defense if an armed attack occurs against a Member of the United Nations, until the Security Council has taken measures necessary to maintain international peace and security."

Article 51 clearly applied to the United States. Japan was not a Member of the U.N. in 1951, but after regaining its sovereignty it, too, would have the inherent right of self-defense.

38. Interview with Nishimura.

39. The negotiations also involved the Peace Treaty, but the following pages focus on the Security Treaty, which seems to have occupied the major place in the discussions. Gerald L. Curtis, "Dulles-Yoshida Negotiations," in *Columbia Essays in International Affairs,* II (New York: Columbia University Press, 1967), 50. Curtis writes: "Dulles' appointment calendar indicates that he met with Yoshida on five separate occasions during the little more than two weeks he was in Japan. It was during these meetings that final compromises were hammered out concerning a separate security pact and Japanese rearmament."

Both sides quickly agreed that the security arrangements should be concluded separately from the peace treaty. At first, Ambassador Dulles seemed rather receptive to the Japanese draft treaty, but within a few days it became clear that his approach to the security treaty was radically different from Prime Minister Yoshida's. For Ambassador Dulles was not satisfied with the National Police Reserve. He was still urging rearmament, by which he meant the building of Japanese ground forces to 350,000 men, capable of repulsing a Soviet invasion.[40] Moreover, although Prime Minister Yoshida and Ambassador Dulles both wanted collective defense, they did not agree on what it meant. Ambassador Dulles, with the recently concluded NATO Treaty in mind, was a strong advocate of regional security. He argued that Japan's safety was dependent on the peace and stability of the Far East, and that Japan should contribute positively to the defense of the entire region.[41]

This was Ambassador Dulles' *quid pro quo.* The United

40. Nishimura, "Seiritsu Jijō," pp. 209, 210. When interviewed, Mr. Nishimura used the figure of 350,000 men. This figure is corroborated in Tatsumi Teruichi, "Saigunbi to Yoshida-san no Gankosa" [Mr. Yoshida's Stubbornness on Rearmament], in Yoshida, *Kaisō Jūnen*, III, 180–81. General Tatsumi, who was military attaché to Mr. Yoshida when the latter was ambassador in London in the 1930s, describes in his article an incident in January, 1952, when he was requested by the Americans to persuade Prime Minister Yoshida that an army of 325,000 men was necessary for Japan's security. When asked about General Tatsumi, Mr. Nishimura recalled that he was on the military advisory group mentioned above, and had assisted Prime Minister Yoshida on military affairs in an unofficial capacity throughout the Yoshida era. The 325,000–350,000-man figure also appears in Kichi Miyazawa, *Tōkyō-Washington no Mitsudan* [Tokyo-Washington Secret Talks] (Tokyo: Jitsugyo no Hi Sha, 1956), p. 191. Mr. Miyazawa used the figure in reference to talks with the United States Government in 1953 and again in 1954 (Ikeda-Robertson talks), at which he was present. Also corroborated in Haji Fumiō, *Ningen Ikeda Hayato* [The Man Ikeda Hayato] (Tokyo: Noma Shōichi, 1967), p. 189. The figure also appears in *The United States in World Affairs, 1953*, p. 265.

According to Tatsumi and Haji, the United States was urging a 325,000–350,000-man army of ten divisions based on the United States Army Table of Organization and Equipment (TO&E), which called for over 30,000 men in a division. Haji writes that at the 1954 Ikeda-Robertson meeting, Ikeda agreed to ten divisions, but based on the Japanese TO&E of less than 20,000 men to a division, which added up to a ground force of 180,000 men.

41. Nishimura, "Seiritsu Jijō," pp. 207–9.

States would be willing to cooperate in the defense of Japan if Japan immediately began taking vigorous measures to defend itself and would agree to participate militarily in regional security. He did not believe that Japan was economically and psychologically incapable of rearming. Nor did he think that Article IX was an insurmountable obstacle.[42] He took no notice of the internal-external security equation, and he would not be satisfied with Japanese pledges for continued economic, political, and even military cooperation—cooperation of the kind Japan was then giving the United States in the Korean War.

The touchstone of Ambassador Dulles' position, to which he repeatedly made reference, was the Vandenberg Resolution, passed by the Senate in June, 1948, as the basis for United States participation in NATO. That resolution stated that the United States would associate with such "regional and other collective arrangements as are based on continuous and effective self-help and mutual aid." He warned that the Senate would not ratify the security treaty unless it met the requirements of this resolution, and he insisted that "continuous and effective self-help and mutual aid" meant military self-help and military action.[43]

Prime Minister Yoshida argued that Japan was doing and would undertake to continue doing all it could, within the limits of its economic resources and its Constitution, to defend itself and to cooperate with the United States in maintaining regional security. But he would not move on the rearmament

42. Interview with Nishimura. On this point, the bad feeling between Prime Minister Yoshida and Mr. Ashida mentioned above (p. 54n) seems to have intruded into the negotiations. Mr. Nishimura, who was present at the negotiations, explained that Prime Minister Yoshida thought that Ambassador Dulles' tough stance on rearmament had been influenced by Mr. Ashida's broad interpretation of Article IX. Moreover, Prime Minister Yoshida came to believe that the Americans were making Mr. Ashida privy to the negotiations, despite an understanding that they were to be kept confidential. Mr. Nishimura thought that Prime Minister Yoshida's suspicions on these matters contributed to the friction which developed during the negotiations.

43. Interview with Nishimura.

issue. He insisted that rearmament on the scale urged by Ambassador Dulles was impossible,[44] and that consequently Japan would not, for the foreseeable future, be able to commit itself to military action beyond its own shores.

Prime Minister Yoshida and Ambassador Dulles were strong-minded men. The negotiations took on a bitter, unpleasant tone. Neither side felt it could compromise on the rearmament issue, and it seemed that the talks would end in failure. Then someone, it is not clear who, suggested that perhaps the impasse on rearmament could be resolved with General Mac-Arthur's advice. Together, Prime Minister Yoshida and Ambassador Dulles met with General MacArthur. The General agreed with the Prime Minister. General MacArthur did not believe that it was either possible or desirable for Japan to undertake a program of large-scale rearmament. Ambassador Dulles was loath to take on General MacArthur in an argument on military affairs. He backed away from his insistence on immediate rearmament, and tried for a Japanese commitment for future rearmament.[45]

Prime Minister Yoshida would not agree to undertake any formal commitment for rearmament in the treaty, either immediately or in the future. But he did soften his position by pledging verbally that Japan, within the limits of its economic

44. Nishimura, "Seiritsu Jijō," p. 210. Yoshida, *Memoirs*, p. 267, and Tatsumi, *Kaisō Jūnen*, III, 180–81. In a television interview in 1965, Mr. Yoshida told of a stormy three-hour meeting with Dulles in which he was presented with a demand for rearmament. According to this account, Mr. Yoshida told Mr. Dulles not to joke (*jōdan iu na*), and pointed out that the Japanese people did not have enough to eat. Moreover, he argued that if he were to agree to rearmament, his Government would fall, and that anyone who carried out rearmament as a result of Dulles' order would be killed as a traitor. "Yoshida Shigeru ga Kataru Gaikō Hiwa" [Yoshida Shigeru Relates the Secret History of His Foreign Policy], transcript of NHK television interview, August 29, 1965, *Heibon Panchi*, September 20, 1965, p. 20.

45. Nishimura, "Seiritsu Jijō," pp. 210, 211. In *Heibon Panchi*, September 20, 1965, p. 17, Yoshida relates that Mr. Dulles had an appointment with General MacArthur and suggested that Mr. Yoshida accompany him. According to Mr. Yoshida, he happily consented, because he had received General MacArthur's agreement beforehand to support him in his position on rearmament and, if necessary, to dissuade Mr. Dulles from insisting on rearmament.

resources and its Constitution, would make every effort to build forces for its own defense against direct and indirect attack.[46] Mr. Dulles put as much of this verbal pledge as he could into the preamble to the treaty, but he still would not go along with the provisions in the Japanese draft for consultation and cooperation under the United Nations Charter, and for an American guarantee. He argued that until Japan actually rearmed there could be no realistic basis for cooperation.[47] If Prime Minister Yoshida wanted the United States to defend Japan until Japan was able to defend itself, the United States would do so, but only on its own terms and as part of its wider effort to protect the security of the entire Far East. Moreover, despite Prime Minister Yoshida's protests, Ambassador Dulles insisted that the provision for the possible use of American forces to protect Japan's internal security be inserted in the treaty.[48]

The only point on which Prime Minister Yoshida and Ambassador Dulles were really in agreement was on the necessity of stationing United States forces in Japan after the conclusion of the peace treaty. Consequently, this was the only formal obligation that appeared in the treaty. The rest of the text is a statement of expectations, intentions, and hopes, and reads more like a press communiqué than a contract. Mr. Nishimura's carefully fashioned "silk hat" was lost. The mutual, cooperative defense arrangement and the explicit American guarantee called for in the Ashida memorandum and desired by Prime Minister Yoshida were not realized. But Prime Minister Yoshida did get an implicit, *de facto* guarantee in the form of the base agreement.

The Ashida memorandum had not anticipated either the Korean conflict or Ambassador Dulles. The Korean conflict

46. Yoshida, *Memoirs*, p. 267. Interview with Nishimura.
47. Interview with Nishimura.
48. *Ibid.* It should be noted that the text of the Security Treaty was written during negotiations in the spring and summer of 1951 (see Nishimura, *Jōyaku Ron*, p. 31). Mr. Nishimura stated, however, that the substance of the treaty was hammered out in the January negotiations.

changed the strategic assumption behind the proposal for emergency-use bases and led Prime Minister Yoshida to conclude that the retention of United States forces in Japan would be necessary in order to protect Japan's security interests in Korea. Then Ambassador Dulles' insistence on rearmament and participation in regional defense as the price of a mutual treaty and a guarantee forced Prime Minister Yoshida to sign a treaty which did not provide for mutuality, in order to get the necessary guarantee, *de facto*.

Although Prime Minister Yoshida was only partially successful in realizing the goals of the Ashida memorandum in the 1951 Security Treaty, his failures did not result from a change of heart or a lack of effort. On the contrary, considering the obstacles he encountered, he did well to get the necessary American *de facto* guarantee, without committing Japan to large-scale rearmament or to a military responsibility for regional defense. Moreover, as subsequent events were to show, Prime Minister Yoshida came away from the negotiations with Ambassador Dulles still determined to make the defense arrangements mutual, by which he meant that the two Governments would consult and cooperate for the defense of Japan. But the negotiations convinced him that a mutual defense agreement would only be possible if Japan started to build its own forces for defense against external attack. The external-internal security equation was not abandoned, but Prime Minister Yoshida realized that it would not be enough.

FOUR

ᘓᘓᘓᘓᘓᘓᘓᘓ

Security Treaty Diplomacy, 1952–1957

I

FROM 1951 until the signing of the Treaty of Mutual Cooperation and Security in 1960, the Japanese Government applied itself to realizing those provisions set forth in the draft treaty prepared by Mr. Nishimura Kumao in the fall of 1950, which Prime Minister Yoshida had tried but failed to have written into the first Security Treaty.[1] Specifically, the Government sought to:

1. Place the security arrangements squarely within the framework of the United Nations Charter.

2. Gain an *explicit* guarantee from the United States of Japan's external security.

3. Obtain an agreement establishing a United States–Japanese consultative committee for the purpose of regulating the use of the United States military bases in Japan and coordinating the two Governments' views on questions pertaining to the defense of Japan.

4. Ultimately, to replace the 1951 Security Treaty with a new treaty which would include the above, and which would also include provisions for a fixed duration for the treaty and more conventional arrangements for extending and terminating it. And finally, to eliminate from the new treaty any reference to possible American intervention for maintaining internal security.

1. Mr. Robert D. Murphy, ambassador to Japan in 1952–53, was kind enough to read this chapter. In an interview on October 31, 1968, Mr. Murphy said that he considered Section I to be an accurate description of the attitude and the policy of the Japanese Government toward the Security Treaty during his ambassadorship.

Prime Minister Yoshida and the Foreign Ministry officials concerned with the treaty made a clear distinction between the first three items and the last item. The former could be achieved through agreements supplementing the 1951 Security Treaty and would be given first priority. The latter could only be realized by making a new treaty, and would have to be postponed at least until the war in Korea was settled.[2] Although disappointed by the results of the January, 1951, negotiations, the Japanese officials comforted themselves with the thought that the treaty was vague and provisional. It could be developed by interpretation, and it had been concluded with the understanding that it would be replaced by a mutual treaty.

True, Ambassador Dulles' position had been that a new treaty would be negotiated only when Japan had rearmed. But Prime Minister Yoshida believed that there was room for maneuver on the rearmament issue.[3] Officially, the Americans were pressing for the building of Japanese forces of approximately 350,000 men. Prime Minister Yoshida considered that figure to be out of the question. As will be seen in this chapter, and in greater detail in the next, he was willing to expand and reorganize the National Police Reserve and to add to its mission of maintaining internal security the task of participating in Japan's external defense. But neither he nor his successors have ever undertaken to build the forces thought necessary by the Americans at the time of the Korean War. The Japanese Government's policy has been to get the security arrangements it wanted by compromising on the rearmament issue, and by practicing a patient, skillful diplomacy intended to encourage the Americans to withdraw gracefully from the position taken by Ambassador Dulles in the 1951 negotiations.

One of the basic premises of Prime Minister Yoshida's policy

2. Interview with Nishimura.
3. Kōsaka, *Saishō Yoshida Shigeru*, pp. 43–47. Haji, pp. 187–89. Tatsumi, *Kaisō Jūnen*, III, 180–81.

(and of the Ashida memorandum) was that Japan had to base its defense on cooperation with the United States. But Japan had no way to coerce or pressure the United States into co-operating. The only way to get American cooperation was to ask for it on matters in which it was clearly in America's interest to cooperate. In short, all depended on the United States Government perceiving that the defense of Japan was vital to American interests. In 1947, it had appeared that the United States Government might fail to make this basic perception. That Government had seemingly ignored Prime Minister Yoshida's informal feelers early in the year, as well as Foreign Minister Ashida's memoranda on security in the summer and fall. And as late as February, 1949, Assistant Secretary of the Army Kenneth C. Royall had held an informal press conference during a visit to Tokyo at which he stated that Japan would be indefensible in a war with the Soviet Union, and that American forces should be withdrawn from Japan and deployed to Europe, where they would be of more use. Although promptly repudiated, Mr. Royall's remarks filled the Japanese Government with doubts about United States policy toward Japan.[4]

From the Royall incident until the 1951 negotiations with Ambassador Dulles, however, Prime Minister Yoshida was satisfied with the direction of United States policy. It reflected a continually increasing awareness of the value of having a stable, secure, and prosperous Japan for an ally in the Far East. And the war in Korea confirmed, beyond a reasonable doubt, the seriousness of the United States commitment to Japan's defense.

When he encountered Ambassador Dulles in the Security Treaty negotiations, however, Prime Minister Yoshida realized that there was a danger that the war in Korea was leading the Americans to exaggerate the Soviet-Communist threat in

---

4. Van Aduard, p. 103. Harry Emerson Wildes, *Typhoon in Tokyo* (New York: MacMillan Company, 1954), p. 291.

the Far East, and to overreact to it. There were moments in the 1951 negotiations when Ambassador Dulles, arguing for rearmament, seemed to be saying that a Soviet attack on Japan was imminent. Moreover, Prime Minister Yoshida felt that there was a strong idealistic, crusading strain in Ambassador Dulles' approach to the security arrangements. Ambassador Dulles seemed to believe that the Red menace would produce miracles. Confronted with the Communist threat, Japan and its former enemies and colonies were supposed to become allies overnight. The Japanese people, recently defeated and demoralized in a terrible war, and completely demilitarized by the American Occupation authorities, were supposed simultaneously to rebuild their shattered economy and stage a rapid, large-scale rearmament. Moreover, it was extremely difficult for Prime Minister Yoshida to counsel restraint, to tell Ambassador Dulles that he was exaggerating the threat and asking for too much to counter it, when American soldiers were suffering heavy casualties in Korea, just across the narrow straits of Tsushima.[5]

But Prime Minister Yoshida believed that, given time and a closer knowledge of Far Eastern affairs, Mr. Dulles and those who thought as he did in the United States Government would realize that the regional security arrangements which were appropriate to Western Europe could not be applied to Northeast Asia, and that American interests in the Far East did not require the building of large Japanese armed forces. Moreover, Prime Minister Yoshida thought that Ambassador Dulles had made a tactical error in the negotiations when he made rearmament the price of mutuality.[6] For mutuality was as necessary for the United States as it was for Japan. The Americans, after all, had agreed to maintain more than six hundred military bases and facilities in the country after

5. Interview with Nishimura.
6. Nishimura, "Seiritsu Jijō," p. 213. Mr. Nishimura emphasized this point during his interview.

Japan regained sovereignty.[7] Prime Minister Yoshida viewed these bases as an effective guarantee of Japan's external security, and as being necessary to the protection of Japan's interests in Korea. He was also aware, however, that the United States Government considered the bases to be vital to the preservation of American interests in the Far East. In order to use the bases, the Americans would require the co-operation and support of the Japanese Government and people. And the obvious and sensible way to continue to get that cooperation and support was to meet and consult with Japanese officials, and to persuade them that the bases were being used as the Japanese wanted them to be used. In practice, consultations had begun even before the Peace and Security Treaties came into effect in late April, 1952, and they would become increasingly frequent and more concerned with substantive issues with the passage of time.

Consequently, although Prime Minister Yoshida was not satisfied with the 1951 Security Treaty as a legal document, he was confident that in practice it would satisfy Japan's basic security requirements. Nevertheless, he was determined to get the guarantee and the arrangements for consultations put into writing. He and his successors believed that explicit, public agreements would strengthen the United States–Japanese security system and would help to avoid misunderstandings between the two Governments. Moreover, and of equal importance, they wanted formal, written agreements for domestic political use. The 1951 treaty was too vulnerable to criticism. To its critics, it seemed to give military bases to the United States, without extracting from the United States a commitment to defend Japan. And it seemed to leave the United States free to use these bases just as it wanted to, without

7. In 1954 there were approximately 200,000 U.S. servicemen and 630 U.S. military installations in Japan, including bases, training areas, depots, warehouses, and communication facilities. *Bōei Nenkan, 1955* [Defense Yearbook] (Tokyo: Bōei Nenkan Kankō Kai, 1955), p. 78.

taking into account Japan's interests.[8] It would not be enough to tell the critics of the treaty that the Americans could be trusted to defend Japan and not to misuse the bases.

This, then, is the background against which Japan's defense policy was conducted in the 1950s. It was still following the basic lines set forth in the 1947 Ashida memorandum, as incorporated in the Nishimura draft treaty of 1950. The 1951 Security Treaty was viewed as a partial, implicit realization of the American guarantee and the mutual defense arrangements. The task before the Japanese Government was to have the guarantee made as clear, firm, and explicit as possible; to formalize and define the areas of consultation and action for the defense of Japan; and eventually to negotiate a more satisfactory, mutual treaty. The means to these ends were to be limited rearmament and friendly persuasion.

II

PRIME MINISTER Yoshida showed his good faith on the rearmament issue soon after the Peace and Security Treaties came into effect in late April, 1952, by announcing the reorganization of the 75,000-man National Police Reserve into the National Safety Agency, to be composed of a 100,000-man National Safety Force and an 8,900-man Maritime Safety Force. These forces were not expressly authorized to defend Japan against external attack, but during 1952 and 1953 they gradually assumed partial responsibility for the defense of Hokkaido, replacing elements of the United States Seventh Cavalry Division.[9]

8. These criticisms run through most of the Japanese commentaries and analyses of the treaty, including those by its supporters—including Mr. Nishimura—who attempt to counter the criticisms. An excellent account in English of the opposition to, and criticism of, both the 1951 and 1960 treaties is George R. Packard III, *Protest in Tokyo* (Princeton: Princeton University Press, 1966).

9. *Jieitai Jūnen Shi* [Ten-Year History of the Self-Defense Forces] (Tokyo: Okurasho Insatsu Kyoku, 1961), pp. 53–55.

While compromising on the rearmament issue, the Yoshida Government took steps to make the American guarantee more explicit and to define and formalize consultations under the Security Treaty. Between July and December, 1952, Soviet MIG-15 fighter planes operating from Sakhalin and the southern Kuriles violated Japan's territorial air space over Hokkaido approximately fifty times,[10] obviously conducting reconnaissance flights, and probably testing the effectiveness of the United States–Japanese security arrangements. These overflights were observed and reported by American forces in Hokkaido, and also by the Japanese police. The Yoshida Government considered the overflights to be a serious threat to Japan's security, and since the Japanese had no means of repelling them, it wanted the United States to take action.[11] The question was, What kind of action?

Prime Minister Yoshida and Foreign Minister Okazaki Katsuō did not want to instigate an American-Soviet air war over Japan. Moreover, there was still the rearmament question to consider. If they made too much of a fuss over the Soviet reconnaissance flights, they would be undermining their own argument on the nature of the Soviet threat to Japan and generating pressure for the rapid, large-scale rearmament program they were trying to avoid.

The United States Government, represented in Tokyo by Ambassador Robert D. Murphy and General Mark W. Clark, commander in chief, Far East Command, also had reason for restraint. General Clark has written that his mission included the defense of Japan against external attack, and that the Soviet reconnaissance flights were compromising the security of his forces in Hokkaido.[12] But the primary theater of military

10. *Asahi Shimbun* (Asahi Newspaper), January 13, 16, 1953. From a Foreign Ministry source.
11. Interview with Mr. Murphy.
12. Mark W. Clark, *From the Danube to the Yalu* (New York: Harper and Brothers, 1954), p. 126: "The Presidential directive which outlined my mission in Japan was explicit in delegating me to direct contact with the

operations during 1952 was Korea, and he probably did not want to divert large numbers of aircraft from the United Nations Command to Hokkaido.

Consequently, both Governments were able to agree on a limited and cautious response to the Soviets. The occurrence of the overflights was kept out of the newspapers through the summer and fall, and General Clark gradually reinforced the United States air forces in Hokkaido with a number of F-86 Sabrejets. Then, after a flurry of overflights in December, the intrusions suddenly stopped. The Sabrejets had intercepted the MIGs and had made it clear to the Soviets that their violations of Japanese air space would not go unchallenged.[13] In brief, the two Governments had consulted, as Prime Minister Yoshida had expected they would, the American guarantee had been invoked, and it had proved effective. So far, so good.

There remained, however, the possibility that the Soviets might renew their intrusions, perhaps in greater force, thus increasing the danger of combat over Hokkaido. In order to warn the Soviets that future intrusions would, if necessary, be forcefully repelled, and at the same time to make it clear that American military action against the Soviet MIGs had been requested by the Japanese Government, and that such action would not violate Japan's sovereignty, the two Governments agreed to issue a public warning to the Soviets and to publicize the overflights.[14] On January 13, 1953, Foreign

Japanese Government in matters pertaining to the defense of the country. My basic responsibility was to defend Japan against any possible external attack. At the time that meant Soviet Russia, which had bases within a few miles of the Japanese northern coastline. Defense of Japan was one of my most serious missions in the Far East, a mission that was vital to the security of the United States.

"It was my responsibility too, to encourage the Japanese to build a defense force and train it to be an effective anti-invasion army."

13. Interview with Mr. Yasuda Hirō, chief, Legal Section, Defense Agency, on April 4, 1968. Although Mr. Yasuda could not permit me to use the Defense Agency file on the Murphy-Okazaki Notes, he referred to that file to answer my questions.

14. Interview with Mr. Yasuda. This is also the gist of the Foreign Ministry statement in *Asahi Shimbun,* January 17, 1953.

Minister Okazaki sent a formal note to Ambassador Murphy in which he stated:

Violations of Japan's territorial air over Hokkaido by foreign military planes have of late become increasingly frequent. The Japanese Government considers that such trespasses are not only forbidden under international law but also constitute a grave menace to the security of Japan. The Japanese Government does not possess at present any means effectively to repel such violations.

I have the honor, therefore, to request your Excellency on behalf of the Japanese Government that, if similar violations of Japan's territorial air should occur in future, the United States authorities concerned take effective and appropriate measures to repel them for the protection of the common interest of Japan and the United States of America.[15]

On the same day, the Foreign Ministry called a press conference at which it released this note and made public the history of the overflights.[16]

On January 16, Ambassador Murphy formally replied, acknowledging Foreign Minister Okazaki's note and stating:

In accordance with the request of the Japanese Government, the United States Government has instructed the Commander in Chief, Far East Command, with all practicable assistance from the Japanese Government, to take all possible measures necessary and proper under terms of the Security Treaty . . . to repel all such violations of Japan's territorial air.[17]

This note was also immediately released to the press, and General Clark issued a public warning to the Soviets against further overflights. He also publicly ordered an anti-Soviet air patrol over Hokkaido and directed the Sabrejet pilots "to shoot, if and when they contacted Communist MIGs."[18] Ac-

---

15. Headquarters, United States Forces Japan, *United States-Japan Treaties, Agreements and Other Documents*, May 1, 1961, p. 56. Cited hereafter as Hq, USFJ. During the interview with Mr. Murphy, I asked if Mr. Okazaki's note was a Japanese initiative, or if it was suggested by the United States Government. Mr. Murphy answered that he remembered the exchange of notes and their immediate publication as being a Japanese initiative.
16. *Asahi Shimbun*, January 13, 1953.
17. Hq, USFJ, p. 56.
18. Clark, p. 130. *Asahi Shimbun*, January 16, 1953.

cording to General Clark, one MIG-15 challenged his warning, and it was intercepted and shot down. Except for unintentional overflights resulting from navigational errors, that incident seems to have marked the end of Soviet intrusions into Japanese territorial air space.

On the 16th, a Foreign Ministry spokesman also explained the Murphy-Okazaki Exchange of Notes on Air Defense to the press. He said:

The arrangements for United States action were made under Article I of the Security Treaty, in which it was agreed that the United States forces in Japan ". . . may be utilized to contribute to the maintenance of international peace and security in the Far East. . . ."[19]

This spokesman was careful not to quote the rest of this sentence, which is ". . . and to the security of Japan against armed attack from without . . ." because his Government was taking the position that the MIG intrusions were not armed attacks but trespasses. The spokesman then went on to explain:

Under the Security Treaty, the United States has a comprehensive obligation to defend Japan, and therefore it was not necessary for Japan to request American help in each individual case. But under this arrangement [the Murphy-Okazaki Notes], we have set the precedent that *as a matter of principle, unless the Japanese Government requests it, the United States will not take action.* However, this is not to say that the United States will never, under any circumstances, take action to counter a sudden attack unless there is first a Japanese request.[20]

In effect, the Japanese Government viewed the exchange of notes on air defense as an interpretation of the Security Treaty—an interpretation which clarified the American guarantee against direct attack and, in principle, limited American military action undertaken from bases in Japan for the de-

19. *Asahi Shimbun,* January 17, 1953.
20. *Ibid.* Italics added.

fense of Japan to action taken at the request of the Japanese Government. It would be interesting to know how the United States Government, and in particular Secretary of State Dulles, reacted to this explanation of the Murphy-Okazaki Notes. Whatever the Government's reaction was, however, it did not publicly refute the Japanese interpretation. On the contrary, in practice, the Americans seemed to be moving toward a similar interpretation.

III

IN MARCH, 1954, the Yoshida Government concluded the Mutual Defense Assistance Agreement with the United States. The main purpose of the agreement was to establish a proper legal basis for the furnishing of military equipment and technology by the United States to Japan under the Mutual Security Act of 1951, and to clarify the terms of Japan's contribution to the support of the United States forces in Japan. But as its title suggests, the agreement also reflected the Japanese Government's persistence in pursuing its defense policy. The preamble placed the agreement squarely "within the framework of the Charter of the United Nations" and referred to the Security Treaty, stating that it was concluded in order "to promote peace and security in accordance with the purposes and principles of the Charter of the United Nations" [21]—a phrase which the Japanese Government had tried but failed to have inserted into the Security Treaty itself.

Prime Minister Yoshida formally acknowledged his verbal commitment to limited rearmament in Article VII, in which the Japanese Government agreed:

to fulfill the military obligations . . . assumed under the Security Treaty . . . [and to] make, consistent with the political and economic stability of Japan, the full contribution permitted by its man-

21. Hq, USFJ, p. 48.

power, resources, facilities and general economic condition of the development and maintenance of its own defensive strength and the defensive strength of the free world.[22]

In order to emphasize the limitations on the Japanese defense effort, the Government also gained American agreement in the preamble to the stipulation that:

in the planning of a defense assistance program for Japan, economic stability will be an essential element for consideration in the development of its defense capacities, and that Japan can contribute only to the extent permitted by its general economic condition and capacities.[23]

Finally, and perhaps most importantly, in the Mutual Defense Assistance Agreement the United States Government acknowledged that Japan's economic and political cooperation and support, and its limited rearmament program, contributed to the common defense and constituted a proper basis for mutuality in the security arrangements. This was a significant shift from Mr. Dulles' position in the 1951 negotiations, which had made large-scale rearmament and military cooperation in regional defense the basis for a mutual security agreement. The 1954 agreement did not provide for formal consultations on the use of the bases or on general security matters, but it did establish the principle upon which such consultations would be based.

In the summer of 1954, his last in office, Prime Minister Yoshida again reorganized and expanded Japan's armed forces. After a long and acrimonious debate in the Diet, his Government gained approval for the Defense Agency Establishment Law and the Self-Defense Forces Law. These laws created the National Defense Agency and the Ground, Maritime, and Air Self-Defense Forces, with a total authorized strength of 152,110 men.[24] Moreover, according to law, the mission of

22. *Ibid.*
23. *Ibid.*
24. See Table 1, p. 111.

these forces was and is "to defend Japan against *direct and indirect aggression*, and when necessary, to maintain public order."[25] The passage of these laws represented the Government's first official acknowledgment of its responsibility for Japan's external defense.

IV

IN DECEMBER, 1954, Hatoyama Ichiro, leader of the Democratic Party, replaced Mr. Yoshida as prime minister. His Government, which remained in office until December, 1956, was distinguished in foreign affairs by its success in reaching an agreement with the Soviet Union in October, 1956, legally ending hostilities and establishing diplomatic relations; and also for gaining membership for Japan in the United Nations in December of that same year. The so-called Normalization Agreement, in particular, was hailed as a diplomatic triumph in Japan. But Prime Minister Hatoyama and Foreign Minister Shigemitsu Mamoru were well aware of its shortcomings. They had approached the Soviets in the spring of 1955, in an optimistic, friendly spirit, hoping for a peace settlement and a relaxation of international tensions in the Far East. They had planned to conclude a peace treaty with the Soviet Union which would have returned to Japan the northern islands—Kunashiri, Etorofu, Habomai, and Shikotan. But the Soviets had proved intransigent on this as well as on other substantive issues, and eighteen months of grueling negotiations and the limited scope of the Normalization Agreement convinced the Government that the prospects for a rapprochement were dim. Not only had the Soviets refused to budge on the territorial question, but they had also insisted that the price for a peace treaty was abrogation of the Security Treaty with the

25. "Jieitai Hō" [Self-Defense Forces Law], Chapter III, Article 1, in *Bōei Jitsumu Shoroppō, 1967* [Defense Laws] (Tokyo: Naigai Shuppan Sha, 1968), p. 66. Italics added.

United States.[26] Prime Minister Hatoyama wanted a peace treaty with the Soviets badly, but not that badly.

For the defense policy of the Hatoyama Government was a variation on the Yoshida-Ashida theme. Prime Minister Hatoyama continued to base Japan's external defense on the 1951 Security Treaty, but at the same time he attempted to accelerate formal revision of the treaty and lessen its importance to Japan, and in the process establish a more equal, mutual relationship with the United States and greater diplomatic independence. To achieve these ends, he tried to bring about a dramatic improvement in relations with the Soviets, and he was also willing to rearm at a faster pace than Prime Minister Yoshida. During his two years in office, the authorized strength of the Self-Defense Forces jumped to 214,182 men,[27] and their equipment was greatly improved under the Mutual Defense Assistance Agreement. The tone of relations with the United States on security matters was also improved by the reduction of United States forces in Japan from close to 200,000 men in late 1954 to approximately 90,000 men in December, 1956.[28] Although the Eisenhower Administration seems to have made these curtailments in the aftermath of the Korean War and in keeping with its New Look strategy,[29] and not simply at the request of the Japanese Government, Prime Minister Hatoyama got credit in Japan for the cuts. Thus, despite the Hatoyama Government's approach to the Soviets, the Japanese-American security arrangements were not loosened, and because of the greater readiness on the part of the Japanese to rearm, the American officials dealing with Japan found it easier, in certain respects, to cooperate with the Hatoyama Government than with its predecessor.

26. Semi-official accounts of the discussions are in *Bōei Nenkan, 1956,* pp. 131–40. *Bōei Nenkan, 1957,* pp. 171–83. See also, *Asahi Nenkan, 1957* (Tokyo: Asahi Shimbun Sha, 1957), pp. 298–302.
27. See Table 1, p. 111.
28. *Ibid.*
29. Council on Foreign Relations, *The United States in World Affairs, 1956,* pp. 207–9.

The Hatoyama Government, in its eagerness for treaty revision, even showed a momentary willingness to compromise with Secretary of State Dulles' definition of mutuality—something the Yoshida Government had never done. For Prime Minister Yoshida, mutuality had meant only cooperation in the defense of Japan. On August 29–31, 1955, Foreign Minister Shigemitsu visited Washington to clarify his Government's Soviet policy, and to explain Prime Minister Hatoyama's desire for a new security treaty. The United States Government had been quite liberal in interpreting the treaty, but revision proved to be another matter. Secretary Dulles again insisted that if the Japanese wanted a mutual treaty they must rearm to the point where they could defend themselves against a Soviet invasion, and they must be willing to share with the United States the burden of maintaining regional security.[30] The military advisers with Secretary Dulles declared that they no longer saw a need for Japanese ground forces totaling 350,000 men. Changes in weaponry and the decrease in international tension following the conclusion of the armistice in Korea led them to believe that well-equipped Japanese ground forces of approximately 200,000 men would be adequate to protect Japan.[31] At the time of this meeting, the Ground Self-Defense Force numbered approximately 150,000 men. Foreign Minister Shigemitsu indicated that his Government planned to increase the ground forces to 180,000 men by 1958, and he urged that negotiations for a new security treaty be undertaken promptly, on the assumption that this figure would be realized.[32]

Secretary Dulles then raised the question of Japanese participation in regional defense. At first, Foreign Minister Shigemitsu declined to discuss this question, stating that his Government could not even contemplate the dispatch of forces

---

30. *Asahi Shimbun*, August 30, 1955. *The Mainichi*, August 31, 1955.
31. *The Mainichi*, August 31, 1955.
32. *Bōei Nenkan, 1956*, p. 143. *Asahi Shimbun*, August 31, 1955.

overseas until Article IX of the Constitution had been amended. A member of the American delegation suggested that the issue be discussed informally, with no minutes being taken, and Foreign Minister Shigemitsu reportedly agreed.[33] Secretary Dulles then surprised the Japanese by shifting the region to be secured from the Far East (South Korea and Taiwan) to the Western Pacific. He declared that he was not asking Japan to commit itself to the defense of North America, or even Hawaii. But he thought it was only reasonable to expect that Japan share in the defense of Guam.[34]

Confronted with an apparent effort toward compromise by the Americans, and eager to get negotiations started for a new treaty, Foreign Minister Shigemitsu decided to risk a political storm at home. Their joint communiqué reported:

It was agreed that efforts should be made, whenever practicable on a cooperative basis, to establish conditions such that Japan could, as rapidly as possible, assume primary responsibility for the defense of its homeland and be able *to contribute to the preservation of international peace and security in the Western Pacific*. It was also agreed that when such conditions are brought about it would be appropriate to replace the present Security Treaty with one of greater mutuality.[35]

When this communiqué was made public in Tokyo, however, it quickly became apparent that the Hatoyama Government was not going to undertake a military commitment in the Western Pacific, or anywhere else outside Japan. Sunada Shigemasa, then director-general of the National Defense Agency, told reporters that the Defense Agency Establishment Law prohibited the overseas dispatch of members of

33. *Mainichi Shimbun*, September 2, 1955. *Asahi Shimbun*, September 2, 1955.

34. *Asahi Shimbun*, September 2, 1955. See also Kurahara Nobuhiro, *Nichi-Bei Ampō Jōyaku no Shōten* [Focus on the United States–Japan Security Treaty] (Tokyo: Asahi Shimbun Sha, 1967), p. 47.

35. U.S. Department of State, *Bulletin*, September 12, 1955, p. 419. Italics added.

the Self-Defense Forces.[36] The Socialists, and a surprising number of influential Liberals and Democrats (then on the verge of merging into the Liberal Democratic Party), charged the Hatoyama Government with violating the law and the Peace Constitution. The Government in Tokyo seems immediately to have concluded that the communiqué would be too hot to handle. Foreign Minister Shigemitsu, while still in Washington, declared that the communiqué was being misinterpreted. He insisted that he had not committed Japan to any military obligations.[37] After returning home he went even further, announcing before the Foreign Affairs Committee of the House of Councilors that the Government had not undertaken any commitment, military or otherwise, in the Western Pacific. The communiqué, he explained, had simply been an agreement in principle.[38] Following this fuss, Prime Minister Hatoyama seems to have shelved his plans for treaty revision.

V

ON THE OTHER HAND, the Hatoyama Government did succeed in extending Japanese control over the United States bases and in strengthening the consultation arrangements. Specifically, the Hatoyama Government established the precedent, still in effect today, that the United States would not bring atomic or thermonuclear weapons into Japan without the agreement of the Japanese Government. On July 28, 1955, an official spokesman in Washington announced that the United States Army was in the process of deploying atomic cannons to Okinawa and was planning to equip its forces in Japan with Honest John missiles, capable of carrying atomic warheads.[39] It was not made clear in this announcement whether the missiles would be atomic-tipped.

36. *Asahi Shimbun*, September 4, 1955. *Bōei Nenkan, 1956*, pp. 143–44.
37. *Bōei Nenkan, 1956*, pp. 143–44.
38. *Asahi Shimbun*, September 15, 1955. *Bōei Nenkan, 1956*, p. 146.
39. *The Mainichi*, July 29, 1955. AP dispatch.

The Hatoyama Government had been discussing this deployment with the Americans since the previous March [40] and was not at all surprised by the announcement, although it may have been annoyed by its ambiguity. But members of the Diet and the press were shocked. Most Japanese, remembering the horrors of Hiroshima and Nagasaki, were strongly opposed to the presence of nuclear weapons on their soil. On July 29 and 30, the Prime Minister and the Foreign Minister appeared before the Foreign Affairs Committee of the House of Councilors. They explained that, while the Honest John missile could be armed with an atomic warhead, it was also an effective conventional weapon. They gave solemn assurances that the Honest Johns being brought into Japan were not atomic-armed. Prime Minister Hatoyama stated that, at discussions during the previous May between Foreign Minister Shigemitsu and Ambassador John M. Allison, it had been agreed that the United States would consult with the Japanese Government before bringing atomic or nuclear weapons into Japan. He said that in an emergency Japan might want to have these weapons in the country for defense, but that there was no present need for them.[41]

The Honest Johns began arriving in Japan on August 20. The Americans still refused to say whether they were armed with atomic warheads. But following the Government's explanation and assurances, most of the Democrats and Liberals in the Diet rallied behind the Prime Minister, and the press

40. *The Mainichi,* July 31, 1955. UP dispatch. In an interview on July 30, 1955, General John E. Hull, former U.S. Far East commander, stated that on March 25, 1955, he had notified Foreign Minister Shigemitsu of the plans of the United States to equip its forces in Japan with Honest Johns. Moreover, he stated that he had explained that these missiles could be armed with atomic or conventional warheads, and that the United States did not intend to put atomic weapons in Japan except in a war emergency. This same issue of *The Mainichi* reported that, on July 30, Parliamentary Vice-Minister Sonoda Sunao had stated before the Foreign Affairs Committee of the Lower House that the Government had started discussions with the United States on the Honest Johns during the previous March. See also *Bōei Nenkan, 1956,* pp. 176–78.

41. *Asahi Shimbun,* July 30, 1955. *Bōei Nenkan, 1956,* pp. 177–78.

shifted its attention to other matters. The opposition Socialist and Communist parties clung to the nuclear issue, however, and fulminated and led rallies against the Honest Johns with some success right through the winter and into the spring of 1956.

The Honest John incident showed more clearly than the Soviet intrusions over Hokkaido in 1953 that the use of the United States bases in Japan was circumscribed not only by Japanese Government policy but by public opinion as well. Apparently the Eisenhower Administration, as part of its global New Look strategy, planned to equip its forces in Japan with atomic missiles. When informed of these plans in the spring of 1955, the Hatoyama Government opposed the introduction of atomic weapons, arguing that their presence would turn public opinion against the United States and the security arrangements. The Americans seem to have replied that Honest John missiles in Japan were a strategic necessity and that the NATO members were already equipped with them. The upshot was a compromise. The Hatoyama Government agreed to the introduction of the missiles, without the atomic warheads. This would position the missiles and their crews in Japan. If the international situation should deteriorate to the point where both Governments believed the atomic warheads were needed, then the Japanese Government would agree to their being brought into Japan.

The vagueness of the American statements as to whether or not the Honest Johns were atomic-armed was dictated by the strict security regulations governing the deployment of these weapons, and probably also by the American desire to test Japanese public opinion. If there had been no public outcry, or if it had passed more quickly, the United States Government would probably have continued to press for the atomic warheads in Japan. As it was, the anti-atomic furor was even greater than the Hatoyama Government had expected.

As a result, both Governments came to recognize that the

United States bases in Japan would have to be limited to a conventional, supporting role in America's Far East strategy. The necessity for close consultation and cooperation on the use of the bases was reaffirmed. Not only would the Japanese Government be consulted on the deployment of the United States forces stationed in Japan, but it would also have a voice in deciding the weapons with which they were to be equipped.

VI

PRIME MINISTER Hatoyama left office in December, 1956, and following the brief, two-month premiership of Ishibashi Tanzan, was succeeded by Prime Minister Kishi Nobusuke. Prime Minister Kishi's foreign policy was a shift back to the Yoshida approach. Under Kishi, the Japanese Government would not attempt to extend Prime Minister Hatoyama's efforts for a rapprochement with the Soviets. For Prime Minister Kishi was content to seek security, prosperity, and a measure of diplomatic independence for Japan in partnership with the United States, as a loyal member of the Free World.

In defense policy, also, Prime Minister Kishi hewed close to the Yoshida-Ashida line. He had accompanied Foreign Minister Shigemitsu to Washington in 1955 and had not forgotten the fate of the "Western Pacific" communiqué. Under his Government there would be no further hints that Japan might undertake a military role in maintaining regional security. He would continue gradually to build up the Self-Defense Forces and would try to negotiate a new security treaty. For him, as for Prime Minister Yoshida, mutual security meant cooperating in the defense of Japan.

In June of 1957, Prime Minister Kishi visited Washington. The main purpose of his trip was to start negotiations for a new security treaty. He took with him plans for further expansion and improvement of the Self-Defense Forces, but otherwise offered no concessions. Rather, he emphasized

Japan's growing prosperity, stability, and status; the lessening of cold war tensions; and the provisional nature of the 1951 Security Treaty.[42] Six years had passed since the conclusion of that treaty. The fighting in Korea, which had done so much to shape the treaty, had been ended by an armistice in 1953. In 1956, with American sponsorship, Japan had been admitted to the United Nations, resuming full, respected membership in the international community.

Prime Minister Kishi pointed out to President Eisenhower and Secretary Dulles that the 1951 treaty, based as it was on the notion that Japan had no means to defend itself, and that the United States would defend Japan as it saw fit, was clearly out of date. The treaty no longer described the actual security arrangements, and it was a continual source of controversy in Japan. A new, mutual treaty would be in the interests of both Governments and should be promptly negotiated. He urged that the new treaty should: (1) place the security arrangements clearly within the framework of the United Nations Charter; (2) provide for regular, formal consultations on the equipment and deployment of the United States forces in Japan; and (3) be made effective for either ten or fifteen years, after which the treaty could be extended, or terminated by either party.[43]

By 1957, President Eisenhower and Secretary Dulles were ready to agree with most of what Prime Minister Kishi had to say. Japan had not rearmed to the level they had desired, nor had it assumed a military role in regional security. But neither had the NATO members rearmed adequately, and following the 1956 Suez crises, the concept of regional security may have lost some of its magic. Moreover, Japan had staged an extraordinary economic recovery and had become a more stable, self-reliant, and cooperative ally than had been ex-

---

42. *New York Times,* June 22, 1957. *Asahi Shimbun,* June 23, 1957. Kurahara, pp. 50, 51.

43. Kurahara, pp. 50, 51.

pected in Washington when the Security Treaty was concluded in 1951. Secretary Dulles could assure himself that
the 1951 treaty had been a good piece of work at the time.
But he himself had declared that it should be provisional, and
now it needed revising. Finally, there was a chance that the
Japanese Government, given a new, mutual treaty, might see
its way toward accepting a more positive, active role in maintaining the security of the Far East.[44]

President Eisenhower and Secretary Dulles were willing to
begin preparatory talks which might lead to negotiations for a
new treaty, but they did not want publicly to commit themselves to negotiations. In the joint communiqué issued at the
close of this meeting, the two Governments announced the
beginning of a "New Era" in Japanese-American relations,
based on equal partnership and close cooperation. These words
were given some substance in the communiqué by an agreement to establish a joint committee on security, which would
discuss all matters relevant to the implementation of the
Security Treaty.[45] Questioned by the press, Secretary Dulles
admitted that the committee might even discuss revision of
the treaty.[46] On August 6, 1957, the Japanese-American Committee on Security came into existence, composed of the
Japanese Foreign Minister and the Director-General of the
Defense Agency, and the United States Ambassador to Japan
and the Commander in Chief, Pacific, or his alternate, the
Commander, United States Forces, Japan.

Apparently, Prime Minister Yoshida and his colleagues had
calculated correctly in 1951. Limited, gradual rearmament
and a patient, skillful diplomacy had led the Americans toward
acceptance of Japan's defense policy. This is not to suggest

44. U.S. Congress, Senate, Committee on Foreign Relations, *Treaty of Mutual Cooperation and Security with Japan*, 86th Congress, 2d Session (1960), pp. 8–10, 19–22.
45. Text of communiqué, U.S. Department of State, *Bulletin,* July 8, 1957, pp. 51–53.
46. *Asahi Shimbun,* June 24, 1957.

that the Japanese policy makers in 1947 and in 1951 had been gifted with perfect foresight, or that the United States Government, realizing the truth of Prime Minister Yoshida's strategic perceptions and persuaded by the logic of Japan's diplomats, had become converts to the Japanese Government's policy. On the contrary, as will be noted in the discussion of the 1960 treaty, the United States continued to advocate its conception of mutuality, which continued to rest on regional defense. Moreover, there is little doubt but that the development of nuclear missiles, changes in Soviet policy following Stalin's death, and the New Look strategy—all factors beyond the control of the Japanese Government—contributed to the shaping of United States security policy in the Far East.

In fact, however, a regional defense system for Northeast Asia showed no signs of materializing, the United States had sharply reduced its forces in Japan, and the Japanese Government had not rearmed to the desired level. As a consequence, by the end of the decade the 1951 treaty in practice was operating as a guarantee of Japan's external security, and in the Murphy-Okazaki Notes on Air Defense, that guarantee had, to a limited degree, been made explicit. Moreover, the Notes on Air Defense, the Mutual Defense Assistance Agreement, the Shigemitsu-Allison talks, and the establishment of the Security Consultative Committee all indicate that the United States had found it useful to consult with the Japanese Government on the disposition and equipment of forces in Japan, and that in so doing, the Americans were moving perceptibly closer to the mutual defense relationship which Prime Minister Yoshida had sought in 1951. Following the Kishi-Eisenhower meeting in 1957, it appeared that the United States Government was ready to acknowledge openly this state of affairs by negotiating a new treaty.

FIVE

ᒕᒧᒕᒧᒕᒧᒕᒧ

Defense Policy and the 1960 Treaty

I

THE TREATY of Mutual Cooperation and Security concluded in Washington, D.C., on January 19, 1960, embodies virtually every item included in the draft treaty prepared by Mr. Nishimura Kumao under Prime Minister Yoshida's instructions in the fall of 1950, and represents the realization of the basic ideas of the 1947 Ashida memorandum.[1] In the Preamble, and in Articles I, V, and VII, the security arrangements are placed squarely within the framework of the United Nations Charter, Articles II and IV make provisions for cooperation and mutual aid, and in Article IV the Parties agree to hold consultations "from time to time regarding the implementation of this Treaty, and at the request of either Party, whenever the security of Japan or international peace and security in the Far East is threatened."[2] Article V states:

Each Party recognizes that an armed attack against either Party in the territories under the administration of Japan would be dangerous to its own peace and safety and declares that it would act to meet the common danger in accordance with its constitutional provisions and processes.[3]

1. The writer is especially indebted to Mr. Nishimura Kumao; to Mr. Sezaki Kasami and Mr. Yoshida Shigenobu of the Foreign Ministry, North American Affairs Bureau, Security Treaty Section; and to Mr. Nōda Hidejirō, Foreign Ministry, Asia Bureau, Chief, Northeast Asia Section, for their advice and assistance in preparing this chapter.
2. "Treaty of Mutual Cooperation and Security Between the United States of America and Japan," U.S. Department of State, *Bulletin*, XLII, No. 1072 (February 8, 1960), 185, 186. Cited hereafter as Treaty.
   3. *Ibid.*

It should be noted that, while the Japanese Government agreed in Article IV to consult on matters pertaining to the peace and security of the Far East, in Article V it obligated itself to *act* only in the event of an armed attack against Japan.

Again, as in the 1951 treaty, the *de jure* expression of the American intention to defend Japan against attack is substantiated by a base agreement in Article VI which states:

For the purpose of contributing to the security of Japan and the maintenance of international peace and security in the Far East, the United States of America is granted the use by its land, air and naval forces of facilities and areas in Japan.[4]

Together, Articles V and VI embody the formal, explicit guarantee and the mutuality sought by the Japanese Government since 1947. In these articles, the United States Government formally committed itself to the defense of Japan, and explicitly recognized that the defense of Japan was a matter of common interest and a proper basis for mutuality.

A quick reading of Article V suggests that the basis of mutuality is the obligation of the Parties to act in the event of "an armed attack against either Party." But on closer inspection it becomes clear that the key words in this sentence are "in the territories under the administration of Japan." For as Articles V and VI make clear, United States forces are stationed on Japanese territory, with the agreement of the Japanese Government, for the purpose of assisting in the defense of Japan. An armed attack against the United States forces in Japan would necessarily also be an armed attack against Japan. Thus, the obligation expressed in the phrase "against either Party" represents only a nominal addition to Japan's commitment to act to defend itself.

It should also be noted that while Article V obligates the two Governments to "act to meet the common danger" it does not obligate them to act together. There is no provision in

4. *Ibid.*

the treaty for joint military action. The Japanese negotiators contended that such a provision was likely to run afoul of Article IX of the Constitution.[5] Equally important, from the Japanese Government's point of view, arrangements for joint military action were unnecessary. The American guarantee was seen as an adequate deterrent, in and of itself. The Japanese Government held to this view in 1947, in 1951, in 1960, and it still held to it in 1968.

Although the Japanese Government had finally succeeded in obtaining the guarantee and the mutuality it had worked and waited for, during the negotiations the treaty specialists in the Foreign Ministry were aware of several loopholes in the text that had to be sewn up tight. To begin with, the new guarantee was not, in one vital respect, as firm as the one it replaced. In Article VI the United States was granted the use of bases in Japan, but it was not obligated actually to maintain forces in and around Japan, as it was under the 1951 treaty. In brief, there appeared to be a danger that the United States Government, while leaving the treaty in force, might withdraw its forces at an inopportune moment and seriously weaken the guarantee. Moreover, although Article VI reinforced the guarantee in Article V, it still seemed to leave the Americans free to equip their forces in Japan with any weapons they saw fit, and to deploy these forces anywhere in the Far East, even against the wishes of the Japanese Government. The efforts of the Japanese Government to correct these defects are especially indicative of its efforts to implement Japanese defense policy in the treaty arrangements, and will be examined later in this chapter.

5. Kamimura Shinichi, *Sōgō Kyōryoku Anzen Hoshō Jōyaku no Kaisetsu* [Explanation of the Treaty of Mutual Cooperation and Security] (Tokyo: Jiji Shin Sha, 1965), pp. 38, 56. Mr. Kamimura served as minister in the Japanese Embassy in Washington, D.C., in 1953–54, and as ambassador to Turkey from 1954 to 1958. His book is a detailed, legal analysis of the treaty that draws upon Foreign Ministry files. Kurahara's *Jōyaku Shōten* is also based partially on Foreign Ministry sources and partially on *Asahi Shimbun* files. Foreign Ministry officials consider both books to be useful and reliable discussions of the treaty.

Returning to the treaty itself, the onerous portions of the 1951 document providing for United States intervention to maintain internal security were eliminated as the Japanese wished.[6] The new treaty was concerned only with an "armed attack," meaning an external attack, and made no mention at all of internal security, thus tacitly acknowledging that the matter of internal security was to be dealt with by the Japanese Government, entirely at its own discretion.

Finally, in Article X, the question of how the treaty would be terminated was resolved by an agreement on a fixed term of ten years (1960 to 1970), after which either party was free to terminate the treaty by giving one year's notice of its intention to do so. Unless such notice was given, the treaty was to continue in effect.[7]

II

THE NEGOTIATIONS for the 1960 treaty were conducted in fits and starts through 1958 and 1959, principally in Tokyo, by Prime Minister Kishi and Foreign Minister Fujiyama Aichiro and Ambassador Douglas MacArthur II. The delays stemmed primarily from domestic political problems in Japan. During a special session of the Diet in the fall of 1958, Prime Minister Kishi tried to have the Police Duties Performance Law amended in order to prevent and control labor disorders and violence. The Socialists and Communists resisted what they considered to be an unconstitutional attempt to curb their activities, and they were not alone in their opposition. Much to the Government's dismay, the vague language of the proposed amendment, which seemed to give the police

6. See Treaty. See also Kamimura, p. 101, and Kurahara, p. 75.

7. Kamimura, pp. 104, 105. Kurahara, pp. 223–27. The question of whether the treaty ought to be revised and formally extended for another fixed period, or permitted to remain in effect indefinitely, was debated within the ruling Liberal Democratic Party during the writer's stay in Japan in 1967–68. By the summer of 1968, it seemed clear that the party and Prime Minister Sato favored automatic extension (*jidō enchō*). See, for example, *Asahi Shimbun,* November 6, 7, and 8, 1967.

unnecessarily wide powers reminiscent of those they exercised in prewar Japan, provoked widespread criticism. A nationwide Anti-Police Law Revision Movement was formed, and on November 5 and 7, 1958, four million Japanese demonstrated and staged strikes across the country to protest against the proposed amendment.[8] Moreover, Mr. Kishi was sharply criticized by faction leaders in his own Liberal Democratic Party for what they considered to be his highhanded approach to Police Law revision. Faced with dissension within his own party, the Prime Minister backed away from the proposed changes in the Police Law, suspended substantive negotiations on the treaty, and devoted himself through the winter and spring of 1959 to mending his political fences in preparation for the House of Councilors election scheduled for June of 1959.[9]

Prime Minister Kishi's difficulties over the Police Law are relevant to security policy. His efforts to strengthen the law indicate that, despite Japan's prosperity and apparent stability, he was still concerned over the continuing threat to internal security posed by the labor movement supporters of the Socialist and Communist parties, whose leaders were still preaching revolution. The demonstrations themselves highlighted the willingness of a surprisingly large number of Japanese to express their opposition to the Government, not through the ballot box, but by taking to the streets. In retrospect, the 1958 demonstrations look like a warm-up for the huge demonstrations and riots of 1960.

Hardly had the difficulties over the Police Law begun, diverting the Prime Minister's attention from the treaty, than the negotiations hit a snag on the question of the area to which the treaty would apply. This question had not arisen in 1951, since the old treaty made no provisions for joint consultations or common action, and there had been no need to specify the

8. Kurahara, pp. 59–66. Packard, pp. 102–5.
9. Kurahara, pp. 62–66. Packard, pp. 102–5.

area within which the parties would cooperate. When this issue was first taken up in the negotiations in October and November, 1958, Ambassador MacArthur reiterated Mr. Dulles' 1955 proposal that the treaty should apply to areas in the Western Pacific beyond Japan, to Guam and perhaps to Taiwan.[10] In effect, the United States Government was again seeking a Japanese commitment for a joint effort to maintain regional peace and security, on the grounds that the security of Japan is dependent on the security of its neighbors. Prime Minister Kishi and Foreign Minister Fujiyama balked at this proposal, just as Prime Minister Yoshida had done in 1951. Although Japan had staged an amazing economic recovery and had strengthened its defense forces, the defense laws still prohibited the dispatch of forces outside Japan. Moreover, Prime Minister Kishi and Foreign Minister Fujiyama did not believe that Japan had the political capability of taking military action beyond its own borders. They explained that the Japanese people still had vivid memories of the consequences of Japan's efforts in the 1930s to stabilize the Far East by military means. They were not ready to tolerate another effort in this direction by their Government, even in cooperation with the United States. Moreover, while it is not clear to precisely what area Ambassador MacArthur made reference in his proposal, the Japanese Government also argued that, while Japan's relations with the Republic of Korea and the SEATO powers were slowly improving, the governments concerned would be alarmed at any sign that Japan intended to extend its sphere of military responsibility.[11]

On the other hand, Prime Minister Kishi was concerned over the defense of the Ryukyu and Bonin Islands. Until the United States had captured and garrisoned these islands at the end of World War II, they had been part of metropolitan Japan. In Article 3 of the 1951 San Francisco Peace Treaty,

---

10. Kurahara, p. 59. *Asahi Shimbun*, November 28, 1958.
11. Kurahara, pp. 177–82. Kamimura, pp. 61–68.

the United States had acquired "the right to exercise all and any powers of administration, legislation and jurisdiction over the territory and inhabitants of these islands including their territorial waters." [12] The two Governments agreed that while the United States had gained administrative control over the islands, Japan possessed residual sovereignty, and the United States Government promised that when peace and stability had been established in the Far East, and it was no longer necessary for the United States to station its forces on the islands, they would be restored to Japan. In the meantime, the United States would be free to equip its forces on the islands with whatever weapons it thought necessary and to deploy these forces anywhere in the Far East without having to consult with the Japanese Government.

Prime Minister Kishi was willing to continue this arrangement, but he wanted to reassert Japan's residual sovereignty in the new treaty. One way of doing this would have been to accept a partial responsibility for defending these islands, and from the fall of 1958 until the spring of 1959 he seems to have toyed with the idea of doing so. Again, however, dissension within the Liberal Democratic Party influenced the Government's approach to the treaty. The strongest proponent of the inclusion of Okinawa in the treaty area was Mr. Kono Ichiro, a powerful faction leader who was hoping at the time to succeed Prime Minister Kishi. Mr. Kono's ambition, however, had produced an alliance against him of rival factions, led by Miki Takeo, Ikeda Hayato, Ishi Matsujiro, and Matsumura Kenzo. These were the same men who had been critical of Prime Minister Kishi's handling of the Police Law amendments, and during the winter they gradually took a strong stand against the inclusion of Okinawa and the Bonins in the treaty area, at least until administrative control of the islands was returned to Japan. Caught between the rival factions,

12. "Treaty of Peace with Japan (September 8, 1951)," Hq. USFJ, pp. 1, 2.

Prime Minister Kishi moved away from Kono toward a closer association with Ikeda and Ishi, and in the process adopted their position on how Okinawa was to be dealt with in the treaty.[13] While these maneuvers were taking place, the negotiations were continued at the working level, but no substantive decisions were reached.

Then, despite the rumblings of popular discontent the previous fall, and the bitter intraparty squabbling, the Liberal Democrats did surprisingly well in the Upper House election of June, 1959. Prime Minister Kishi interpreted the election results as a vote of confidence in his leadership. He reorganized his cabinet and again turned his attention to the treaty negotiations. The question of the treaty area was hammered out by Prime Minister Kishi, Foreign Minister Fujiyama, and Ambassador MacArthur during the fall of 1959. As noted, the Japanese Government agreed to consult with the United States on matters relating to the peace and security of the Far East, but it obligated itself in Article V to take action only in the event of an armed attack on "the territories under the *administration* of Japan." No mention was made in the treaty of the Ryukyu and Bonin Islands, but in an Agreed Minute appended to the treaty the Japanese Government expressed "the strong concern of the Government and people of Japan for the safety of the people in these islands *since Japan possesses residual sovereignty over these islands.*" [14]

Thus, the Japanese Government managed to reaffirm its residual sovereignty in the treaty without committing itself to the defense of the islands, and at the same time obtained assurances that if the treaty was still in effect when the administration of the islands was returned to Japan, the United States would continue to share in their defense. It seems fair to conclude that Prime Minister Kishi, despite his domestic

---

13. Packard, pp. 69–81. See also "Tōnai Chōsei Kusuburu" [Smoldering Adjustment within the Party], *Asahi Shimbun*, April 12, 1959.

14. "Agreed Minute to the Treaty of Mutual Cooperation and Security," Hq, USFJ, p. 24. Italics added.

difficulties, steered his way with great skill through the negotiations on the treaty area and Okinawa.

III

THERE REMAINED, however, the problem already alluded to of formally establishing a degree of publicly recognized control over the United States forces stationed in Japan under the treaty. Firstly, it was essential to the Japanese Government that the United States forces not be drastically reduced or completely withdrawn, unless the Japanese so wished. Article VI of the treaty, as already noted, made military bases available to the United States, but it did not obligate the United States actually to man these bases. Secondly, despite the provisions in Article IV of the treaty for consultations, it was still not clear from the text if the Japanese Government would have a voice in deciding whether the United States forces in Japan would be sent into combat areas outside Japan. The Government not only wanted to keep American forces in Japan as long as they were considered necessary; it also wanted to make certain that these forces did not participate in combat operations outside Japan, which might involve them in hostilities without Japanese consent. Thirdly, there was the question of nuclear and atomic weapons. Prime Minister Kishi wanted to formalize the 1955 Allison-Shigemitsu understanding, according to which the United States had agreed not to equip its forces in Japan with atomic or nuclear weapons unless the two Governments first agreed that such a step was necessary.

The Americans were unwilling to clarify these points in the treaty text. But Prime Minister Kishi and Foreign Minister Fujiyama were successful in arranging for a formal exchange of the following notes, on the day the treaty was signed: [15]

15. "Exchange of Notes Incorporating the Agreed Consultation Formula," Hq, USFJ, p. 19.

(JAPANESE NOTE)

Washington, January 19, 1960

Excellency:

I have the honour to refer to the Treaty of Mutual Cooperation and Security between Japan and the United States of America signed today, and to inform Your Excellency that the following is the understanding of the Government of Japan concerning the implementation of Article VI thereof:

Major changes in the deployment into Japan of United States armed forces, major changes in the equipment, and the use of facilities and areas in Japan as bases for military combat operations to be undertaken from Japan other than those conducted under Article V [in response to an attack against Japan], of the said Treaty, shall be the subjects of prior consultation with the Government of Japan.

I should be appreciative if Your Excellency would confirm on behalf of your Government that this is also the understanding of the Government of the United States of America.

I avail myself of this opportunity to renew to Your Excellency the assurance of my highest consideration.

His Excellency   Nobusuke Kishi
   Christian A. Herter
   Secretary of State
      of the United States of America

(AMERICAN REPLY)

January 19, 1960

Excellency:

I have the honor to acknowledge the receipt of Your Excellency's Note of today's date, which reads as follows:

[text of Japanese note]

I have the honor to confirm on behalf of my Government that the foregoing is also the understanding of the Government of the United States of America.

Accept, Excellency, the renewed assurances of my highest consideration.

Christian A. Herter
Secretary of State
   of the United States of America

His Excellency
   Nobusuke Kishi
   Prime Minister of Japan

In another set of notes exchanged on the same day, the Japanese-American Committee on Security, set up in August, 1957, was renamed the Security Consultative Committee, and was designated as a channel for the implementation of Articles IV and VI of the treaty, including the Prior Consultation Notes.[16]

President Eisenhower clarified the intent behind the Prior Consultation Notes, and reinforced them, in the joint communiqué issued immediately after the conclusion of the treaty. According to the communiqué:

The Prime Minister discussed with the President the question of prior consultation under the new treaty. The President assured him that the United States Government has no intention of acting in a manner contrary to the wishes of the Japanese Government with respect to matters involving prior consultation under the treaty.[17]

The question of whether the United States Government understood prior consultation to mean prior agreement was clarified in the Senate hearings before ratification of the treaty. Senators J. W. Fulbright and George D. Aiken probed Secretary Herter on this point, and were told that prior consultation on the subjects of the notes meant the "prior approval of the Japanese Government."[18] Secretary Herter explained that the usefulness of the bases in Japan had always been contingent on the cooperation and support of the Japanese Government and people; that it was not practical to take actions regarding the bases which ran counter to their wishes; and that the prior consultation formula was nothing more than a formal recognition of these facts of life.[19]

16. "Exchange of Notes Re Establishment of the Security Consultative Committee," Hq, USFJ, p. 23.
17. Text of communiqué, U.S. Department of State, *Bulletin,* XLII, No. 1072 (February 8, 1960), 186.
18. U.S. Congress, Senate, Committee on Foreign Relations, *Treaty of Mutual Cooperation and Security with Japan,* 86th Congress, 2d Session (1960), pp. 10, 20.
19. *Ibid.,* pp. 20, 21.

The Prior Consultation Notes have not, to date, been publicly invoked. One can only speculate on how effective they would be in warding off a major reduction of the United States forces in Japan if, for instance, the American Government, for economic or military reasons, should ever decide on a cutback. As a restraint against the introduction of nuclear weapons, however, the formula has certainly been honored. In practice, the United States Government has gone further than required by the notes in deferring to the wishes of the Japanese. Both Governments have agreed that, under the treaty, United States ships of war, either nuclear or conventionally powered, are free to visit Japanese ports without prior consultation.[20] But knowing how sensitive many Japanese are with regard to all things nuclear, the United States Government did not send the U.S.S. *Nautilus*, a nuclear-powered, conventionally armed submarine, into a Japanese port until November, 1963, and then only after months of consultations had taken place and the port call had been publicly authorized by the Japanese Government.[21] The same procedure of consultations and public authorization was followed in arranging the port call of the nuclear-powered aircraft carrier U.S.S. *Enterprise* to Sasebo, in January, 1968.

The only instance of public disagreement between the two Governments over the application of the prior consultation formula occurred shortly after the *Enterprise* visit, in February, 1968, when, following the capture by North Korea of the electronic intelligence vessel, the U.S.S. *Pueblo,* Foreign Minister Miki Takeo expressed concern before the Diet that aircraft assigned to the United States forces in Japan might have been transferred to Korea without prior consultation.[22] A spokesman for the Department of State announced, in reply, that South Korea was not a combat area, that the transfer of

20. Kurahara, pp. 205, 206. Kamimura, p. 76.
21. *Bōei Nenkan, 1964,* pp. 129–31. *Asahi Nenkan, 1964,* pp. 96, 97.
22. *Asahi Shimbun,* February 15, 1968.

aircraft from Japan to Korea was not a "military combat operation," and that such a transfer did not, therefore, require prior consultation.[23] The issue then disappeared from the newspapers, to be quietly settled between the two Governments on the basis of their common interest in the defense of South Korea.

For the Japanese Government, although still not ready to discuss the matter publicly, continued to believe that the defense of South Korea was vital to the security of Japan. In still another set of notes exchanged on that busy day the treaty was signed, the Japanese Government agreed to the continuance in effect of the 1951 Acheson-Yoshida Notes. In those notes, it will be recalled, the Japanese Government had pledged itself to permit the use of the United States bases in Japan for the support of the United Nations Command in Korea. In the 1960 notes, this pledge was reaffirmed and was placed within the framework of the new treaty.

The use of the facilities and areas by the United States armed forces under the Unified Command of the United Nations established pursuant to the Security Council Resolution of July 7, 1950 (for operations in Korea), and their status in Japan *are governed by arrangements made pursuant to the Treaty of Mutual Coopera-tion and Security.*[24]

This meant that the prior consultation formula would apply to the deployment of United States forces in Japan to Korea, and probably explains why the Department of State, in replying to Mr. Miki's remarks on the transfer of aircraft to Korea, took care to note that Korea was not a combat area and that the transfer of the aircraft in question did not constitute a "military combat operation."

Relations between the Japanese and South Korean Governments have slowly, but perceptibly, improved since the days of Prime Minister Yoshida and President Syngman Rhee. In

23. *Ibid.*, February 16, 1968. *Japan Times*, February 17, 1968.
24. Hq, USFJ, p. 22. Italics added.

1965, the two Governments finally established diplomatic relations with one another, and concluded agreements on fishery rights, property claims, and the legal status of Koreans in Japan. Commercial relations between the two countries have since grown rapidly, but there is still no direct cooperation between their Governments on security matters. They cooperate, if the word can be used at all, only indirectly through the medium of their security relationship with the United States.

From the point of view of the Japanese Government, the operational, as distinct from the deterrent, function of the United States bases in Japan continues to be to provide support for the United Nations Command in Korea. In a nutshell, the American bases in Japan serve a dual purpose in Japanese defense policy. They are a convincing symbol of the American commitment to defend Japan against external attack, whether nuclear or conventional. But their operational mission is to support the United Nations Command in Korea, which, from the Government's point of view, remains the first line of Japan's defense. This suggests that the question of how to deal with the American bases in the future—whether to phase them out, or to have only emergency-use bases (as first proposed in the Ashida memorandum)—will be approached by the Government in terms of how many and what kind of United States bases in Japan are necessary to the defense of South Korea.

IV

TAKEN TOGETHER, the 1960 treaty, the Prior Consultation Notes, and the related notes and minutes represent the realization of the security arrangements with the United States which successive Japanese Governments had been seeking since 1947, and which had not been obtained in the 1951 treaty. The United States was formally committed to the defense of

Japan against external attack. The American guarantee was given substance by the presence of United States forces in and around Japan, which were also capable of supporting the United Nations Command in Korea, should such support again become necessary. Japan, much stronger and more stable than expected in 1947 or 1951, was, it is true, obligated to take action to defend itself against an external attack, as well as against domestic disorders and insurrections. But the Japanese Government had not undertaken any military responsibilities outside Japan, and it had gained a decisive voice in the equipping and deployment of the United States forces in Japan.

In short, the Treaty of Mutual Cooperation and Security was mutual in Prime Minister Yoshida's meaning of the word, rather than Secretary Dulles'. The United States and Japan had become partners in the defense not of the Far East, or the Western Pacific, but partners in the defense of Japan and, to a limited degree, the Republic of Korea.

V

THE TWIN GOALS of mutuality and an American guarantee set forth in the Ashida memorandum and persistently pursued by Prime Ministers Yoshida, Hatoyama, and Kishi were intended to satisfy two sets of requirements: (1) the necessity of seeing to it that the defense arrangements with the United States defended Japan as the Japanese Government wanted it defended; and (2) the need for a security policy that would satisfy the voters. For throughout the postwar period, the Conservatives who have governed Japan have acted in the belief that most of the voters have wanted their country to be peaceful, secure, and independent, but would not tolerate a large, costly military establishment or overseas military responsibilities. From the vantage point of domestic politics, the American guarantee and the United States forces stationed

in Japan have been intended to provide peace and security
without rearmament and overseas commitments. Mutuality has
been intended to satisfy the desire for independence, the
natural desire of the Japanese people to believe that their fate
is being decided in Tokyo, not in Washington. As a glance at
the popular reaction to the security treaties suggests, however, selling these carefully made security arrangements to
the voters has been an extremely difficult and slippery task.

In 1951, when Prime Minister Yoshida got his *de facto*
guarantee under relatively onerous terms and without a visible
shred of mutuality, the public acquiesed tamely and rewarded
him with victories in the general elections of October, 1952,
and April, 1953. Nevertheless, deeply concerned that the 1951
treaty might someday be their undoing at the polls, Mr.
Yoshida and his Conservative successors spent the next nine
years revising it. In 1960, Prime Minister Kishi crowned their
efforts with a new treaty that embodied all the provisions
Prime Minister Yoshida had sought in 1951 to please the
voters, especially the provisions for mutual cooperation and
action within the framework of the United Nations Charter
and prior consultation.

The result, however, was not ringing popular acclaim for
this success but the huge protest demonstrations and riots
against the new security treaty centering in Tokyo in May
and June, 1960, which drove Prime Minister Kishi from office.
It can be argued—and has been—that the 1960 demonstrations
were protests against Mr. Kishi's timing, tactics, and personal
style, and not against the treaty itself.[25] Nevertheless, Prime
Minister Ikeda Hayato (July, 1960, to November, 1964) was
careful to play down the Security Treaty, in the belief that it
was not popular and was best kept out of sight. Prime Minister

25. See Packard, pp. 327–51, for a well-documented summary of various
Japanese and American interpretations of the 1960 crisis. For the view that
the struggle was basically aimed at the treaty, see Shinobu Seizaburo, *Ampō
Tōsō Shi* [A History of the Security Treaty Struggle] (Tokyo: Sekai Shoin,
1961), pp. 495–502.

Sato Eisaku (November, 1964, to the present) has been less hesitant to discuss the treaty and defense policy in public, but he, too, has approached these subjects more cautiously than the prime ministers of the 1950s.[26] The public stance of Prime Ministers Ikeda and Sato indicates that the Treaty of Mutual Cooperation and Security has not won the popular support its authors hoped for.

On the other hand, it is well to remember that the Conservatives have managed to remain in power in Japan continuously since 1948, despite their badly understood and unpopular defense policy, and that successive Conservative Governments have succeeded brilliantly in getting the kind of security arrangements they have wanted with the United States.

26. During 1967 and 1968, Prime Minister Sato attempted to make a more positive defense of the treaty, but he did not approach the forthrightness and boldness (perhaps rashness) of Prime Ministers Yoshida and Kishi. In his speeches on the treaty and on Okinawa, Mr. Sato urged his countrymen to cultivate their "defense consciousness" (*bōei ishiki*). He said that Japan needed military defense, and that until the Japanese were more able and willing to defend themselves, they would have to continue to rely on the treaty and the United States nuclear umbrella. For examples, see *Asahi Shimbun*, August 17 and September 4, 1967. It should also be noted that following the House of Councilors election on July 7, 1968, in which their party retained a strong majority, Prime Minister Sato and Secretary-General of the Party Fukuda Takeo declared that their election victory was a mandate for the Security Treaty. *Japan Times*, July 9, 1968.

SIX

꘠꘠꘠꘠꘠꘠꘠

Defense Policy and the
Self-Defense Forces

I

THE PURPOSE of this chapter[1] is neither to recount the
history of the Japanese armed forces since World War II nor
to analyze in detail their organization and equipment.[2] It is

1. The writer is indebted to Mr. Saeki Kiichi, president, Nomura Research Institute and former Commandant of the National Defense College;
to Mr. Kaihara Osamu, secretary-general of the National Defense Council;
to Mr. Kishida Junnosuke, Mr. Sakanaka Tomohisa, and Mr. Takase Shoji,
of the Asahi Newspaper Security Policy Research Council; to Mr. Ishii
Makoto, Yomiuri Newspaper, International Problems Research Committee;
to Mr. Hata Ikuhiko and Mr. Momoi Makoto, professors at the National
Defense College; to Mr. Kotani Hidejiro and Mr. Wakaizumi Kei, professors of international relations at Kyoto Industrial University and authors of
numerous books and articles on defense policy; and to Mr. Nishihiro Seiki,
Defense Agency, Defense Bureau, for their advice and assistance in preparing this chapter.

2. There are no substantial published studies in English on Japan's
armed forces, perhaps because the Self-Defense Forces have played an un-
spectacular and subordinate role in Japanese policy. Among the articles
available, however, are James H. Buck, "The Japanese Self-Defense Forces,"
Asian Survey (September, 1967), pp. 597–613; Alvin D. Coox and Yoshitaka
Horie, "Japan's Self-Defense Force Today," *Marine Corps Gazette* (February, 1965), pp. 50–53; Martin E. Weinstein, "Japanese Air Self-Defense
Force—Restrained but Powerful," *Air Force Space Digest* (December, 1967),
pp. 56–63; and Weinstein, "Defending Postwar Japan," *The New Leader*
(July 3, 1967), pp. 12–15.

See also Weinstein, "The Rebuilding of Japan's Armed Forces" (Unpublished Master's thesis, Department of Public Law and Government and East
Asian Institute, Columbia University, 1965).

In Japanese, there are numerous published sources, including *Bōei Nenkan*,
which provides an unusually complete annual account of military develop-
ments in Japan, as does *Nihon no Anzen Hoshō* [Japanese Security Policy]
(Tokyo: Anzen Hoshō Chōsa Kai), which has appeared annually since 1966.
Two useful and readily available historical accounts are Sakanaka Tomohisa
et al., *Nihon no Jiei Ryoku* [Japan's Self-Defense Power] (Tokyo: Asahi
Shimbun Sha, 1967), and Doba Hajime, *Nihon no Gunji Ryoku* [Japan's
Military Power] (Tokyo: Yomiuri Shimbun Sha, 1963).

rather to examine the role of the armed forces in Japan's defense policy—the policy conceived in 1947 and developed and modified through the 1951 and 1960 security treaties with the United States.

In 1947, the Government, first under Prime Minister Yoshida and then under Prime Minister Hatoyama and Foreign Minister Ashida, decided that United States–Soviet conflict was inevitable; that neutrality or reliance on the United Nations for military security was impractical; and that Japan, already under an American-controlled occupation, should, after regaining its sovereignty, cast its lot with the United States. The Government anticipated that the Soviets would attempt to draw Japan away from its association with the United States and into the Socialist camp by instigating and supporting Communist-led riots and insurrections, and also by threatening or actually launching a direct attack from the north, through Hokkaido.

Mr. Yoshida and Mr. Ashida had believed that, if permitted to build paramilitary, centralized police forces, the Japanese Government would be able to handle the internal threat itself. And given the superiority of United States naval and air power, they believed that a direct Soviet attack could be deterred by a United States guarantee of Japan's external security, by maintaining bases in Japan for emergency use by the United States, and by the stationing of United States forces in the areas adjacent to Japan, which at that time probably meant in the Ryukyu and Bonin Islands. In the 1947 Ashida memorandum, the Japanese Government proposed to implement this defense policy through a mutual defense agreement with the United States, under which the two Governments would consult and cooperate in the defense of Japan.[3]

The Government believed then that Japan's strategic value to the United States, Japan's willingness to assume complete responsibility for the internal Communist threat, to cooperate

3. See ch. 2, above.

with the United States in external defense, and to remain in close political and economic association with the United States, constituted a realistic and reasonable basis for a mutual defense arrangement.

Thus, the original role planned for the Japanese armed forces was both military and diplomatic. These forces were to maintain internal security, and by so doing were to contribute to the creation of a mutual defense relationship with the United States, which was to include a guarantee of Japan's external security. Mr. Yoshida and Mr. Ashida did not want simply to hand Japan's security problems over to the United States, which would have meant making Japan into an American military dependency. They anticipated that it would be a matter of vital interest to the United States to prevent a Communist take-over in Japan. They thought that such a take-over was as likely to result from subversion and insurrection as from direct attack. By undertaking to build adequate internal security forces, and to make available in Japan emergency-use bases, they were, from their point of view, offering to share with the United States in the task of defending Japan.

In 1947, neither SCAP nor the United States Government seems to have payed much attention to the Japanese Government's proposals for post-peace treaty security arrangements. And as already noted, despite the abortive general strike of February 1, 1947, continuing labor disorders and violence, and requests by Prime Minister Yoshida, General MacArthur, until the outbreak of the Korean War in the summer of 1950, continued to refuse the Japanese Government permission to build internal security forces. It was not until July, 1950, when the bulk of the American units based in Japan were on their way to fight in Korea, that he finally authorized Prime Minister Yoshida to establish the 75,000-man National Police Reserve.

When Prime Minister Yoshida met Special Ambassador

Dulles in the January, 1951, Security Treaty negotiations, he proposed a mutual defense agreement along the lines set down in the Ashida memorandum, except that instead of emergency-use bases he offered to make available to the United States whatever installations were necessary for the conduct of the United Nations operation in Korea. *Despite the Korean War, the role which Prime Minister Yoshida envisaged for the Japanese forces was still limited to the maintenance of internal security.* Mr. Dulles, however, insisted that a mutual defense agreement would be possible only if Japan rearmed to the level where it could assume primary responsibility for defending itself against a direct Soviet attack, and also could participate militarily in protecting regional security. He urged the rapid expansion of the National Police Reserve into a 350,000-man army.

Prime Minister Yoshida refused to rearm on the scale urged by Mr. Dulles. The upshot of their disagreement was the provisional 1951 Security Treaty, which was not a mutual agreement and which satisfied neither side at the time, although it did provide for the stationing of United States forces in Japan, forces which were a *de facto* guarantee of Japan's external security.

Essentially, the disagreement on rearmament between Prime Minister Yoshida and Ambassador Dulles derived from their different estimates of the nature of the external Soviet threat. Ambassador Dulles seems to have believed that a Soviet invasion of Japan was a distinct possibility, and that it would take all the naval and air forces the United States could spare, since its forces might also be occupied elsewhere, plus a 350,000-man Japanese army, to defend Japan against such an invasion. Prime Minister Yoshida, on the other hand, did not think that the Soviets were likely to undertake an amphibious attack against Japan so long as the Americans remained committed to the defense of South Korea, continued to enjoy naval and air superiority around Japan, and were willing to guarantee Japan's security. As he saw it, an American guarantee would *deter* a Soviet attack, and such a guarantee was the key to Japan's external defense. If the Americans would undertake this commitment, Japan would be safe from direct attack. He believed that, without such a guarantee, Japan in 1951 was too weak economically and in spirit to cope with Soviet Russia, or to build the army Mr. Dulles wanted—an army which he considered unnecessary if the American guarantee was forthcoming.

Nevertheless, although he was unwilling to accept Mr. Dulles' arguments, the Security Treaty negotiations did convince Prime Minister Yoshida that he would have to compromise on the rearmament issue in order to build the mutual relationship he wanted with the United States. He had no intention of building forces capable of participating in regional defense, or even capable of assuming primary responsibility for external security. But he did decide to expand the National Police Reserve from an internal security force into an armed force capable of participating in Japan's external defense.

Thus, in the spring of 1952, when the Peace Treaty and the Security Treaty came into effect, Prime Minister Yoshida reorganized and expanded the National Police Reserve into the National Safety Agency, composed of the 100,000-man National Safety Force and the 8,900-man Maritime Safety Force. While the National Safety Force was not explicitly authorized to wage war against a foreign invader, elements of it were deployed to Hokkaido, where they replaced American units responsible for defending the island against a Soviet attack. And in July, 1954, Prime Minister Yoshida pushed the Defense Agency Establishment Law and the Self-Defense Forces Law through the Diet. These laws again reorganized and expanded the armed forces, and explicitly authorized them "to defend Japan against *direct and indirect aggression,* and when necessary, to maintain public order." [4]

4. *Bōei Jitsumu Shoroppō, 1967,* p. 66. Italics added.

In 1954, the actual strength of the combined Ground, Maritime, and Air Self-Defense Forces was 146,285 men. They were equipped with United States World War II vintage machine guns, mortars, recoilless rifles, armored personnel carriers, trucks, and a small number of propeller-driven aircraft, destroyer escorts, and patrol boats.[5] The Self-Defense Forces were adequately equipped to carry out their internal security mission. They were, however, prepared to play only a minor role in Japan's external defense, which was being taken care of by the United States forces in South Korea, in the Western Pacific, and in Japan itself, where close to 200,000 American servicemen, including combat infantry units, were still stationed.[6] This is not to say that the Self-Defense Forces were merely an instrument of the Government's Security Treaty diplomacy. They did reflect Japan's determination to fight in its own defense, and if the Soviets had attempted a landing on Hokkaido in 1954, they would have been met by Japanese as well as by American forces. But the role of the Self-Defense Forces in defense policy, although widened by law to include external defense, was still in practice very similar to that projected in the Ashida memorandum. Militarily, their primary function was internal security. Diplomatically, they were a compromise intended to gain for Japan the mutual security arrangements and the explicit guarantee which the Government wanted from the United States.

II

THE ARGUMENT of this chapter is that the role of the National Defense Agency and the Self-Defense Forces in Japan's defense policy in the late 1960s was still essentially what it was in 1954, and that this limited role continues to reflect the Government's estimate of external and internal threats

5. *Bōei Nenkan, 1955*, pp. 227–47.
6. *Ibid.*, p. 249.

and its judgment on the armed forces required to counter those threats. Diplomatically, the role of the armed forces has shown no significant change. Prime Ministers Hatoyama and Kishi gradually built up the Self-Defense Forces in order to replace the 1951 Security Treaty with the improved 1960 Treaty of Mutual Cooperation and Security. Prime Ministers Ikeda and Sato have continued that gradual build-up in order to maintain the mutuality and the explicit guarantee gained in the new treaty. But the Self-Defense Forces are obviously more powerful than they were in 1954, and the argument that their military role in defense policy remains essentially unchanged requires a more detailed exposition.

After fourteen years of gradual growth the Self-Defense Forces were clearly larger and better equipped than they were in 1954 (see Table 1). Their total strength in 1967 was 231,438 men—156,025 Ground Self-Defense Force, 36,716 Maritime Self-Defense Force, 39,619 Air Self-Defense Force, and 78 Joint Staff Council. Their inventories included the latest-model Type-61 tanks, heavy artillery, transport helicopters, F-104 supersonic jet fighters, Nike Hercules antiaircraft missiles, and forty destroyers and destroyer escorts especially equipped for antisubmarine warfare.[7] And since the American military presence in Japan had been drastically reduced from more than 200,000 men in 1954 to 36,400 in 1967, it is tempting to conclude that the Japanese armed forces have assumed primary responsibility for external defense.

In their public statements, the Government and the Defense Agency make a practice of dodging this question by saying that the defense of Japan is a joint Japanese-American responsibility under the Treaty of Mutual Cooperation and Security.[8] However, in a National Defense Council staff paper

7. *Bōei Nenkan, 1968*, pp. 264–314. See also *Asahi Nenkan, 1968*, pp. 316–18.

8. For instance, see *Nihon no Anzen Hoshō, 1967*, pp. 73–78, and Jiminto Anzen Hoshō Chōsa Kai [Liberal Democratic Party Security Research Committee], *Nihon no Anzen to Bōei* [Japan's Security and Defense] (Tokyo: Izumi Sho Bō, 1966), Part II, ch. IV, pp. 266–79.

TABLE 1

Personnel Strength of the Self-Defense Forces (SDF) and of United States Forces in Japan (USFJ)

	Authorized strength of SDF	Actual strength of SDF	United States forces in Japan
1954	152,110	146,285	210,000
1955	179,769	178,290	150,000
1956	197,182	188,030	117,000
1957	214,182	210,603	87,000
1958	222,102	213,830	77,000
1959	230,935	214,682	65,000
1960	230,935	206,001	58,000
1961	242,009	209,015	48,000
1962	243,923	215,649	46,000
1963	243,923	212,904	45,000
1964	246,094	216,218	46,000
1965	246,094	225,450	40,000
1966	246,094	226,640	34,700
1967	250,372	231,438	36,400

NOTE: Authorized and actual strength of the SDF for 1954–59 is from *Jieitai Jūnen Shi* [Ten-Year History of the SDF] (Tokyo: Okurasho Insatsu Kyoku, 1961), p. 271; for 1956–67, from *Nihon no Anzon Hoshō, 1968*, pp. 366, 367. These are official Defense Agency figures.

Strength of United States forces in Japan is from *Jieitai* [SDF] (Tokyo: Asahi Shimbun Sha, 1968), p. 266.

The discrepancy between authorized and actual strength of the SDF is accounted for almost entirely by deficiencies in the Ground SDF. Because of Article IX of the Constitution, there is no compulsory military service, and all SDF members are volunteers. For more detailed analysis of personnel problems, see Weinstein, "The Rebuilding of Japan's Armed Forces," pp. 16–18.

prepared in 1966 and intended for limited circulation within the government, the military role of the Self-Defense Forces is set forth in greater detail.[9] According to this staff paper, which still embodied the policy of the National Defense Council and the Defense Agency in the summer of 1968,[10]

9. "Waga Kuni Bōei Ryoku no Kihon to Bōei Ryoku Seibi no Arikata" [The Basis of Japan's Defense Power and a Program for Defense Equipment], October, 1966. This document has also been given limited circulation among journalists, and was a basic source, although not cited, for the description and analyses of the missions of the Self-Defense Forces in Sakanaka, *Nihon no Jiei Ryoku*.

10. Interviews with Mr. Kaihara Osamu, secretary-general of the National Defense Council, on April 2 and June 5, 1968.

Japan's security in the late 1960s and the early 1970s is endangered by three kinds of threats.

Firstly, Japan is presently threatened by Soviet nuclear missiles, and in the 1970s it may also face a nuclear missile threat from Communist China.[11] Secondly, there is the threat of conventional, local war, which is most likely to take the form of attacks by the Soviet Union. And thirdly, there is the threat of large-scale internal disorders, which can develop into a "war of national liberation," led by Japanese Communists and supported by Communist China and perhaps the Soviet Union. This last threat is seen as most likely to materialize if war were to break out again in Korea.[12]

For countering the nuclear missile threat, Japanese policy is to rely entirely on the United States strategic deterrent. For maintaining internal security, the policy is to rely entirely on the police and the Ground Self-Defense Forces. For countering conventional attacks, the Government's policy, again, is

---

11. It should be noted that during the 1960s the defense policy planners in Japan viewed the Soviet and Chinese threats in terms of capability rather than intention. As a consequence, although defense policy vis-à-vis Communist China was given considerable attention, the Chinese threat was rated as distinctly smaller than the Soviet. The two aspects of Chinese capability that received the most attention were (1) the progress of China's nuclear weapons program and (2) the possibility that Mao's brand of Communism and his insurrectionary tactics would be adopted and applied by the Communists and left-wing Socialists in Japan. The defense planners, of course, took cognizance of the Sino-Soviet rift. Their reaction, however, was skeptical and cautious. They generally agreed that so long as the dispute continued it reduced the chances of a Soviet attack on Japan. But they felt, especially after 1966, that conditions in China were highly unstable, and that the rift could be quickly closed by a sudden, unpredictable change in Peking's policy. See Kotani Hidejirō and Tanaka Naokichi, "Nihon no Anzen Hoshō no Tenbō" [The Prospects for Japan's Security Policy], in *Nihon no Anzen Hoshō* [Japan's Security Policy] (Tokyo: Kajima Kenkyū Jo Shuppankai, 1964), pp. 753–87 and 908–17. *Nihon no Anzen Hoshō, 1967*, pp. 37–40, 44–51, 161–76. Saeki Kiichi, *Nihon no Anzen Hoshō* (Tokyo: Nihon Kokusai Mondai Kenkyū Jo, 1966), pp. 60–64. Tanaka Naokichi, *Kaku Jidai no Nihon no Anzen Hoshō* [Japan's Defense Policy in the Nuclear Age] (Tokyo: Kajima Kenkyū Jo Shuppankai, 1967), pp. 118–27. Kishida Junnosuke *et al.*, *Chūgoku no Kaku Sen Ryoku* [Communist China's Nuclear War Power] (Tokyo: Asahi Shimbun Sha, 1967). Doi Akio, *Shin Senryaku to Nihon* [The New Strategy and Japan] (Tokyo: Jiji Tsushin Sha, 1968), pp. 155–76.

12. "Waga Kuni Bōei," pp. 1–4.

one of cooperation with the United States, within the framework of the Security Treaty. But the defense planners recognize that the conventional external threat covers a wide spectrum of hostile actions, ranging from infiltration of guerrillas, weapons, and supplies for insurrectionary forces in Japan up through amphibious probing attacks, air attacks on Japanese cities, and interdiction of Japanese shipping, all the way to a full-scale invasion from the north.[13]

The Ground, Maritime, and Air Self-Defense Forces acting together are believed to be strong enough to prevent infiltration and to repel probing attacks. The air defense network, built around the electronic Base Air Defense Ground Environment (BADGE) system, the F-104 jet fighter-interceptors, the Nike Hercules missiles, and antiaircraft artillery, can play an important role in conventional air defense, but only so long as the Self-Defense Forces have adequate fuel and ammunition, which depend on imports by sea.[14] The defense planners anticipate, however, that the Maritime Self-Defense Forces, aided by the Air Self-Defense Forces, could only protect Japanese shipping against submarine, surface, and air attacks in the territorial and coastal waters, and to a very limited degree in the peripheral seas. This means that if air attacks were combined with interdiction of shipping, Japan could not be defended unless the United States employed its naval and air forces in the Pacific and Indian Oceans to keep open the shipping lanes to Japan.[15]

As for the last contingency, a large-scale invasion from the north, the National Defense Council and the Defense Agency recognize that the Self-Defense Forces are not prepared to cope with it. Officially, the Self-Defense Forces are supposed to have two months' reserve ammunition. But according to

13. *Ibid.*
14. *Ibid.* Sakanaka, pp. 52, 53. *Nihon no Anzen Hoshō, 1967*, pp. 193–202.
15. Sakanaka, p. 59. "Waga Kuni Bōei," p. 6.

informed officials, the reserve ammunition figures are computed on an unrealistically low rate of consumption, and they estimate that in actual combat the reserves would probably be used up in a week or less.[16] In effect, the Government still relies on the American guarantee to deter a large-scale conventional attack. The Government believes that if such an attack were to occur, it could only be repulsed by a rapid and equally large-scale American intervention. If such a response were not forthcoming, or were to prove ineffective, the last line of defense would be a protracted guerrilla war against the invader led by the Government.[17]

To sum up, the Japanese defense planners believe that the Self-Defense Forces are capable of handling internal security, preventing infiltration, repelling probing attacks, and playing an important role in Japan's air defense and a minor role in protecting Japan's essential shipping. But despite their growth since 1954, and despite the reduced American military presence in Northeast Asia, the Self-Defense Forces have not assumed primary responsibility for external defense. They have, instead, developed a capability to repel the lesser forms of external attack. This capability is intended to reduce the likelihood that small-scale attacks will be made, and by so doing to increase the probability that a Soviet or Communist Chinese thrust against Japan would be on a large enough scale to activate the security treaty and provoke an American response.

In the jargon of the strategists, the function of the Self-Defense Forces is to raise the threshold of attack. In simpler language, their role in external defense is to strengthen the American guarantee. It should be noted that, as in 1947 and 1951, the Japanese Government still apparently views that guarantee primarily as a deterrent, and only remotely as a

16. This point is also made, somewhat less strongly, in Sakanaka, p. 52, where the estimate is that "the ammunition reserves would last no more than two weeks."
17. "Waga Kuni Bōei," pp. 4, 5.

fighting defense. The dominant view among those concerned with defense policy in the Government is that neither the Soviets nor the Communist Chinese are likely to attack Japan so long as the United States holds up its end of the nuclear balance, remains committed to the defense of South Korea, and maintains the naval and air superiority in the Western Pacific necessary to sustain that defense. Given this favorable disposition of American forces, they believe that Japan can be secured from external attack by an explicit American guarantee reinforced by the threshold-raising Self-Defense Forces.

Several thoughtful critics of the Government's policy have argued that, given the favorable disposition of American forces in the Far East, Japan would be as safe from attack without American bases in Japan and the Security Treaty guarantee as with them.[18] The Government's position is seldom presented in public,[19] but what it amounts to is a belief that the United States forces in Japan are an essential element in the American military position in the Far East, and that the deterrent value of the American forces is much greater if there is an explicit guarantee than if there is not. The Government's position does not directly challenge the argument that the United States would come to Japan's defense even without a security treaty. Its view, rather, is that the treaty and the bases, by clarifying the American intent to defend Japan, serve to prevent an attack. In short, the Government's policy on external defense rests on its conviction that an ounce of deterrence is better than a pound of liberation.

18. For example, see Rōyama Michio, "Kaku Senryaku no Igi to Nihon no Shōrai" [The Meaning of Nuclear Strategy for Japan's Future], *Chūō Kōron* (March, 1968), pp. 50–67. See also the record of a colloquium by Etō Shinkichi, Hoshino Yasusaburo, Kishida Junnosuke, and Murakami Kaoru, "Sekai Senryaku to Nihon no Anzen Koso" [World Strategy and Japan's Security], *Gendai no Me* (Tokushu) (August, 1967), pp. 89–101.

19. For example, see Saeki Kiichi, "Ajia no Anzen to Nihon" [Japan and the Security of Asia], *Kyokutō no Anzen Hoshō* [The Security of the Far East] (Tokyo: Izumi Sho Bo, 1968), pp. 9–36. Nagai Yōnosuke, "Japanese Foreign Policy Objectives in a Nuclear Milieu," *Journal of Social and Political Ideas in Japan*, V, No. 1 (April, 1967), 27–42.

III

ONE MIGHT suppose that Japan's phenomenal economic growth in the 1950s and the 1960s and its apparent political stability signified the disappearance of the internal security threat which so exercised the Government in the poverty-stricken, chaotic period extending from the surrender to the end of the Korean War. There is no doubt that the present Government of Prime Minister Sato appears less likely to be overthrown by labor disorders or by a Communist-led coup than did the Yoshida Government of 1947. The mood of the labor movement, mellowed by Japan's prosperity, is less revolutionary. The Communists and radical Socialists are divided and weakened by internal disputes which have been aggravated by the Sino-Soviet split. And the police and the Self-Defense Forces are much better prepared to maintain internal security than they were during the Occupation and immediate post-Occupation years.

Nevertheless, the Hatoyama, Kishi, Ikeda, and Sato Governments have continued to take the internal threat seriously, and throughout the 1950s and and 1960s the Self-Defense Forces, in particular the Ground Self-Defense Forces, have been equipped, deployed, and trained to maintain internal security.[20] It is true that in the late 1950s, when the first Defense Build-up Plan (1958–61) was being put into effect, the Defense Agency deemphasized the internal security mission as a consequence of its push to develop rapidly an external defense capability. But as Prime Minister Kishi's efforts in 1958 to amend the Police Control Laws suggest, he remained concerned over the internal threat and was anxious to counter

20. The Socialists and the Communists have viewed the Self-Defense Forces since their inception as a militarist-capitalist tool, aimed specifically at them. But their writings on this point, while not entirely devoid of truth, have been marred by ideological stereotypes and exaggeration. A well-informed, relatively detached, and yet critical study of this question appears in Sakanaka, pp. 42–51, 72–86.

it by widening the powers of the police to deal with civil disorders. And whatever apathy may have developed in the Defense Agency toward the internal security mission in the late 1950s was abruptly dispelled by the massive demonstrations and riots of 1960, which led to Prime Minister Kishi's resignation.

Ever since 1960, the Defense Agency and the Self-Defense Forces have shown a renewed awareness of the internal threat and have been preparing to deal with it.[21] During the last two or three years they have been spurred on by the well-publicized intent of the Communists, the revolutionary student groups, and the radical Socialists to succeed in 1970 where they failed in 1960 in "overthrowing" the Government on the issue of whether or not to continue the Security Treaty. The war in Vietnam has led the defense planners to turn their attention from 1960-style disorders which might presage a Communist coup attempt, which they feel confident of being able to prevent, to the problems of dealing with an insurrection in the form of a protracted guerrilla war, probably supported and to some extent directed by Peking and/or Moscow.[22] As already noted, it is anticipated that such a war of national liberation would be likely to accompany the renewal of war in Korea. This was the hypothetical threat being countered in the secret "Three Arrows Plan," news of which leaked out in 1965[23] and caused such a fuss in the Diet and in the press, and this continues to be the major internal threat envisaged by the National Defense Council.

The defense planners do not see this internal threat materializing so long as Japan is prosperous. But as the National Defense Council staff paper implies, and as numerous discussions

21. Sakanaka, pp. 42–51. *Nihon no Anzen Hoshō, 1967,* p. 137. Asahi Shimbun, *Jieitai* (Tokyo: Asahi Shimbun Sha, 1968), pp. 56, 63.
22. "Waga Kuni Bōei," pp. 35–39.
23. Sakanaka, pp. 72–86. For a less sharply focused account in English, see Tsukasa Matsueda and George E. Moore, "Japan's Shifting Attitude Toward the Military: Mitsuya Kenkyu and the Self-Defense Forces," *Asian Survey* (September, 1967), pp. 614–25.

with Japanese of various political persuasions confirmed, it is widely believed by Japanese that their prosperity and stability are extremely fragile. The general strike attempt of 1947 has not been forgotten, and the memory of it was freshened by the French general strike in May, 1968. The defense planners, as well as most economists and businessmen, are convinced that a general strike would cripple the economy in a matter of weeks, and would be likely to undermine the authority of the Government and the parliamentary democracy which it represents. In a somewhat less dramatic but equally disastrous scenario, the defense planners anticipate that the economy could be seriously disrupted either by a prolonged dock worker's strike or a communication worker's strike, either of which would be as effective as interdiction at sea in cutting off the flow of imported fuels and raw materials essential to Japanese industry.

One might suppose that in order to protect the nation from economic collapse the Government could be expected to promptly order the Defense Agency to operate the ports and the railroads. This supposition, however, rests on the further assumption that the public, and in particular the urban industrial and white-collar workers, are basically loyal to the existing parliamentary institutions and would in a crisis uphold the legitimacy and authority of the elected Government. It is exactly this assumption, however, which the defense planners and many other Conservatives as well are not willing to make. For they argue that one third of the voters support the Japanese Socialist Party, and that the Socialists, although not as unabashedly revolutionary as the Communists, are aiming at a peaceful revolution and refuse to accept the legitimacy of the Government.

There is, then, an ambiguity in this approach to the internal threat which reflects the Government's and the Defense Agency's appreciation of the delicately balanced and contradictory elements which hold a political community together, and which make government possible. The defense planners seem to believe that the use of military force to protect the elected Government and the existing institutions may become unavoidable, and that they must be prepared for this contingency. But they do not think that Japan's internal security can be maintained simply by equipping the Ground Self-Defense Forces with helicopters and drilling them in riot control and counterinsurrectionary tactics.[24] On the contrary, they seem painfully aware that the employment of the Self-Defense Forces to settle an economic-political crisis would be an extremely risky and dangerous act, as likely to trigger an insurrection as to prevent one, and as likely to wreck Japan's present political institutions as to preserve them. For the defense planners fear that many Japanese would interpret the use of the Self-Defense Forces as an open admission by the Government that its authority is not respected, and that it can rule only by force. Moreover, even if the Self-Defense Forces were successful in quickly suppressing an internal disturbance, the defense planners expect that many Japanese would interpret this success as a return to a militaristic, authoritarian, prewar government, and they recognize a kernel of truth in this interpretation. For if the government were to become dependent upon the Self-Defense Forces for survival, what would prevent the Self-Defense Forces from dominating the government? True, legally and organizationally the Defense Agency and the Self-Defense Forces are under firm civilian control,[25] and most of the Conservative

24. "Waga Kuni Bōei," p. 75. This point has also been made in a vague way in *Nihon no Anzen Hoshō, 1967*, pp. 47–58, and *Nihon no Anzen Hoshō, 1968*, p. 111.

25. Article LXVI of the Constitution states that "the Prime Minister and other Ministers of State must be civilians." Under the Defense Laws, the Defense Agency is an external organ of the prime minister's office and is subordinate to the prime minister. Moreover, the laws require that the Defense Agency director-general must be a civilian, and the Defense Agency, with only few exceptions, is staffed by civilian officials. The three Self-Defense Forces are headed not by commanders but by staffs, each of which is subordinate to the prime minister and the director-general. The Joint Staff Council,

politicians, businessmen, and bureaucrats, including those in the Defense Agency, seem strongly opposed to a militarist revival. But would the Government be able simply to order the Self-Defense Forces out of politics once they had been called in? Would twenty years of civilian control offset a thousand-year tradition of military rule? [26]

No one, of course, can answer these questions with certainty, and as the following incident suggests, the civilian leaders of the Defense Agency have been reluctant to experiment. In June of 1960, at the height of the Security Treaty crisis, a group of leaders of the ruling Liberal Democratic Party are reported to have asked Defense Agency Director-General Akagi Munenori if he was willing to use the Ground Self-Defense Forces to protect the Diet and executive buildings from invasion by demonstrators and rioters. The party leaders were surprised by Director-General Akagi's response. He was not eager to take action. On the contrary, he replied that, while the Self-Defense Forces had been alerted, he was loath to commit them to action unless the police proved completely incapable of controlling the riots or the confrontation developed into an armed insurrection.[27] Critics of the Government, from both the left and the right, have explained Mr. Akagi's reaction in terms of the Defense Agency's determination to build popular support for the armed forces. The left-wing opposition argued that Mr. Akagi wanted to suppress the disorders, but hesitated to do so because he was afraid to damage the image of "the people's Self-Defense Forces"—an image which is

---

composed of the chiefs of staff, is the highest body of uniformed officers. It functions as an advisory body to the director-general.

Before 1945, the war and navy ministers were officers on active duty and were constitutionally the equals of the prime minister. See Yale C. Maxon, *Control of Japanese Foreign Policy* (Berkeley: University of California Press, 1957).

26. Fujiwara Hirotatsu and Tomita Nobuo, *Hoshu Dokusai no Teihen* [The Foundations of Conservative Despotism] (Tokyo: Bungadō Ginkō Kenkyūsha, 1968), pp. 460–68. Fujiwara and Tomita have analyzed this uncertainty and lack of confidence on the basis of opinion poll data on pp. 193–98 and 273–76.

27. Sakanaka, p. 44. See also Shinobu, *Ampō Tōsō Shi,* pp. 418, 465.

necessary for the rebuilding of the nationalist, militarist spirit upon which a future military take-over must be based.[28] The rightist critics accused the Defense Agency bureaucrats of using the armed forces as a "toy," and of placing their own political ambitions above the safety and order of the country.[29] What is most illuminating is the general agreement that Mr. Akagi's decision to avoid intervening was based on his concern over the popular response to the use of the Self-Defense Forces for suppressing internal disorders.

Given this approach to the internal security question, it is not surprising that in 1968 only four of the thirteen divisions of the Ground Self-Defense Forces were stationed on Hokkaido to protect Japan against external attack, while the remaining nine divisions were deployed in the heavily populated islands of Honshu and Kyushu, close to the major cities and industrial complexes where they could better counter the internal threat.[30] Nor is it surprising that the defense planners take the position that ultimately Japan's security depends on its political stability, which in turn must derive from the sense of national loyalty and patriotism of the Japanese people.[31]

The Self-Defense Forces are the Government's last resort in a showdown with the antiparliamentary opposition. For the Ground Self-Defense Forces, in particular, the maintenance of internal security remains the basic mission. The Government's policy seems to rest on the hope that by being well equipped, carefully trained, and properly deployed, the Ground Self-Defense Forces will prevent the insurrection they are prepared to crush.

28. Shinobu, *Ampō Tōsō Shi*, pp. 418, 465.
29. Hokugo Gentarō (pseudonym), "Kaihara Kambocho no Seppuku" [Secretary-General Kaihara's Suicide], *Gunji Kenkyū* (November, 1966), pp. 132–37.
30. *Bōei Nenkan, 1968.* Map inside front cover shows disposition of all thirteen divisions. Sakanaka, pp. 44–50, 51, discusses troop strength, weapons, training, etc.
31. "Waga Kuni Bōei," p. 74. Sakanaka, pp. 44–50 and Table I-6 on p. 51.

IV

THE CONTENTION that the Government has continued to view the Self-Defense Forces as a necessary but subordinate element in its defense policy is supported not only by its strategic estimates and plans but also, and perhaps more decisively, by its defense budget policy. For an examination of Japanese defense budgets as compared to Gross National Product (GNP) and total government budgets shows that, while the defense budgets have more than trebled ($372 million in 1954 to $1 billion 172 million in 1968), the defense budget has shown a steady decline as a percentage of Gross National Product and total government spending (1.72 percent and 12.87 percent in 1954 to .88 percent and 7.25 percent in 1968; see Tables 2 and 3). The absolute increase reflects the building of the Self-Defense Forces from an internal security force into one capable of participating in external defense, as well as the rising price of modern weapons. On the other hand, the decreasing proportion of the Gross National Product and of the government budget devoted to defense, and the extremely low level of defense expenditures, indicate that the rate of expansion of the Self-Defense Forces has not been pushed to the limits permitted by economic and domestic political considerations.

There is no doubt that public opposition to rearmament and the high priority assigned to economic growth have set limits to the level of defense spending. But the decreasing percentages indicate that defense spending has not approached these limits. For if the war-weary, demoralized, economically insecure Japanese of 1954 could devote 1.72 percent of their Gross National Product and 12.87 percent of their taxes to defense, the revitalized, confident, and increasingly affluent Japanese of 1968 could have done at least as much, if the Government had asked them to.

TABLE 2

Comparison of Japanese Defense Budgets, Government
Budgets, and Gross National Product (in billions of
U.S. dollars)

	Defense budgets (A)	Government budgets (B)	Gross national product (C)	A/B (in percent)	A/C (in percent)
1954	.372	2.89	21.65	12.87	1.72
1955	.356	2.83	24.40	12.58	1.46
1956	.367	2.97	27.48	12.36	1.33
1957	.417	3.30	31.13	12.64	1.33
1958	.410	3.70	31.99	11.08	1.28
1959	.427	4.15	37.16	10.29	1.15
1960	.438	4.90	44.55	8.94	0.98
1961	.503	6.01	53.63	8.37	0.94
1962	.594	7.12	58.86	8.34	1.01
1963	.688	8.49	68.71	8.10	1.00
1964	.780	9.28	79.40	8.41	.98
1965	.848	10.40	87.08	8.16	.97
1966	.959	12.43	101.87	7.71	.94
1967	1.075	14.45	118.56	7.44	.91
1968	1.173	16.16	132.89	7.25	.88

NOTE: Currency conversions have been computed at 360 Yen equals one dollar.

Defense budgets and Government budgets are Defense Agency statistics. The data for 1954–61 were taken from Kotani and Tanaka, p. 941; for 1962–68, from Bōei Nenkan, 1968, p. 350.

Gross National Product figures are Economic Planning Agency (EPA) statistics, extracted from Asahi Nenkan, Economic Sections, volumes for 1964 through 1968. Bōei Nenkan, 1968, p. 350, uses identical GNP figures for 1961–68.

It should be noted that since 1965 the EPA has been using revised methods for computing GNP, which result in higher figures than the pre-1965 methods. For example, the pre-1965 statistics show GNP for 1962 as 39.74 billion dollars as compared to 58.86 billion dollars above. The result of these statistical revisions, of course, is that the percentage of GNP devoted to defense is even less than previously believed. Thus, Nihon no Anzen Hoshō, p. 941, shows A/C for 1962 to be 1.4 percent, while Bōei Nenkan, 1968, p. 350, using the revised GNP figures, shows A/C for 1962 to be 1.01 percent, as does the above table.

TABLE 3

International Comparison of Levels of Defense Expenditures, 1965

Country	Rank	Gross national product as percentage of world total	Defense expenditures as percentage of gross national product
United States	1	29.4	7.6
Soviet Union	2	13.5	8.0
Japan	3	7.5	.9
West Germany	4	5.4	4.4
United Kingdom	5	4.8	5.9
France	6	4.6	5.5
China (Mainland)	7	3.3	7.7
Italy	8	3.0	3.4
India	9	1.7	4.2
Poland	10	1.3	5.5
Sweden	11	1.2	4.4
East Germany	12	1.1	3.8
Czechoslovakia	13	1.0	5.9
Switzerland	14	.7	2.6
Indonesia	15	.6	9.6
Pakistan	16	.4	5.3
South Korea	17	.2	3.9
China (Taiwan)	18	.2	7.7
Thailand	19	.2	2.2
Malaysia	20	.2	4.2

NOTE: This table is compiled from data published by the U.S. Arms Control and Disarmament Agency (ACDA), in *World Wide Military Expenditures and Related Data, Calendar Year 1965*. Ranking of nations by GNP is taken from Table V, pp. 17–19. Defense expenditures as a percentage of GNP are from Table I, pp. 8–12. Conversion of GNP into dollars prior to calculation of GNP as a percentage of world total GNP was based on Purchasing Power Equivalent (PPE). The PPE and the conversions were the work of ACDA consultant Professor Emile Benoit, of Columbia University. Tables for 1965 based on the official rates of exchange rank Japan fifth, behind West Germany and the United Kingdom.

The minor discrepancy between A/C on Table 2 for 1965, which was .97 percent, and the figure on this table, which is .9 percent, is accounted for by ACDA's use of the term *defense expenditures.* ACDA includes only direct military expenditures. Therefore, they based their calculation for Japan on the Defense Agency budget, rather than the total defense budget, which includes rents for United States facilities and other services performed under the Mutual Defense Assistance Agreement of 1954.

Finally, the figures for the Soviet Union and Mainland China are rough estimates.

This is not to suggest that the voters have been willing to amend Article IX of the Constitution, to build nuclear weapons, to raise the Defense Agency to a ministry, or to dispatch Japanese forces overseas, all of which imply huge defense expenditures, the restoration of the prewar military establishment, authoritarian government, and a disastrously aggressive foreign policy. Public opinion polls show that such measures have been highly unpopular.[32] But these same polls also show that a majority of Japanese believe that conventional, strictly defensive forces are necessary, do not violate the Constitution, and are a tolerable tax burden. This suggests that if the Government had wanted to buy more jet fighters, helicopters, destroyers, tanks, or ammunition for the Self-Defense Forces, it could have done so without great political risk.

Moreover, it is hard to believe that Japan's phenomenal rate of economic growth would have been noticeably slowed if defense spending had been held at the 1954 or the 1958 level. But Prime Ministers Hatoyama, Kishi, Ikeda, and Sato permitted the level of defense spending to slip lower and lower, apparently because they were satisfied that their defense budgets met Japan's military needs as these needs were conceived within their over-all defense policies.

There has naturally been disagreement within the Government over the level of defense spending. As one might expect, the Defense Agency has tried to increase its budgets. Annually, the Defense Agency has wrangled with the Finance Ministry over the exact amount of the defense budget. More importantly, the long-range levels of defense spending have been

32. For public opinion poll data on these issues up to 1960, see Douglas H. Mendel, *The Japanese People and Foreign Policy* (Berkeley: University of California Press, 1961), pp. 68–101. For results of more recent polls see Fujiwara and Tomita, pp. 460–68. This book is an analysis of opinion polls including the raw data. Doi Akio, *Shin Senryaku to Nihon* [The New Strategy and Japan] (Tokyo: Jiji Tsushin Sha, 1968), pp. 73–83. Also "Nihon no Bōei—Anata wa Dore o Erabu" [Japan's Defense—What Do You Choose?], *Shūkan Asahi* (April 5, 1968), pp. 22–37. (This last account also includes a well-written note on methods and samplings.)

set in the Defense Build-up Plans, and the available evidence shows that in 1961, when the Second Plan (1962–66) was adopted, and again in 1966–67, when the Third Plan (1967–72) was settled on, the Defense Agency director-generals argued in the National Defense Council and in the cabinet for an increase of defense expenditures up to 2 percent of the Gross National Product.[33] This amounted to a request for a 100 percent increase in the defense budget. The Defense Agency spokesmen pointed to Japan's economic growth, the extremely low levels of defense spending, and the reductions in the United States forces in and around Japan to support their request for a larger portion of the Gross National Product. On both occasions the Defense Agency was opposed by the Finance Ministry, the Ministry of International Trade and Industry, and the Economic Planning Agency, whose spokesmen argued that the present rate of expansion of the Self-Defense Forces satisfied Japan's needs within the Security Treaty framework and fulfilled Japan's obligations under the 1954 Mutual Defense Assistance Agreement; they also argued that a higher rate of defense spending was therefore unnecessary and might interfere with their plans for economic growth.

In both 1961 and 1967 the economic planners prevailed, not simply because economic growth had played a key role in shaping Japanese policy, but also because the Defense Agency director-generals had been unable to convince the prime ministers and their colleagues in the cabinet that 2 percent rather than 1 percent of the Gross National Product was necessary to build and maintain the threshold-raising internal security forces called for in Japan's defense policy. In brief, the economic planners and the Defense Agency spokesmen seem to have been in general agreement on defense policy

33. For an account of the debate in 1961, see Weinstein, "Rebuilding Japan's Armed Forces," pp. 36–39. The 1966–67 controversy is covered in Maeda Hisashi, *Nihon no Bōei Seisaku* [Japan's Defense Policy], Asahi Shimbun Sha Anzen Hoshō Mondai Chōsa Kai 20, July 1, 1967. A less detailed version of this study appears in Sakanaka, pp. 225–62.

and strategy; they have differed only on how much money has been necessary to build forces capable of implementing that strategy. Thus, given the success of the Government's security treaty diplomacy and the apparent effectiveness, to date, of the Self-Defense Forces in carrying out their limited missions, it has been difficult, indeed, for the Defense Agency to make a strong case for a larger share of the budget.

It seems fair to say, then, that the limited role and the small budgets of the Defense Agency and the Self-Defense Forces have not simply reflected the Japanese Government's preoccupation with economic growth and the public's pacifism and opposition to rearmament. On the contrary, the size, equipment, organization, training, and deployment of the Self-Defense Forces have been consistent with the Government's over-all defense policy. The defense establishment has embodied the Government's estimate of the external and internal threats to Japan's security, and its strategic judgment as to what forces have been necessary to counter those threats.

Conclusion

I

LOOKING BACK over the origins and development of Japan's postwar defense policy, it seems clear that this policy was not cooked up in Washington and swallowed whole in Tokyo. While the views on national security articulated in the Diet, in the political parties and pressure groups, and among the Japanese public have been taken into account, the Government's policy has not simply been a response to American initiatives and to pacifist, antirearmament opinion. On the contrary, Prime Minister Yoshida's feelers and Foreign Minister Ashida's memorandum on security policy in 1947 are strong evidence that the Japanese leaders had a well-thought-out defense policy, based on their own strategic views, several years before the United States Government formulated its Far Eastern security policy. Furthermore, the Yoshida-Dulles battle over the 1951 Security Treaty, the way in which that treaty was implemented and finally revised in 1960, and the Government's rearmament policy all indicate that the Japanese leaders have adhered to their policy and gained a large measure of American acceptance for it, while never losing sight of the fact that the success of their policy depended on American cooperation.

II

IN THE CONTEXT of postwar international politics, Japanese defense policy seems relevant on several counts. Firstly, its origins suggest that for the Japanese Government the most pressing foreign policy problem in the aftermath of World War II was to find a way for Japan to exist as an independent political entity in a world dominated by United States and Soviet military power. In Europe the problem does not seem to have appeared as early or with such starkness. For in Europe the United States–Soviet duopoly was not so apparent. Great Britain seemed to count for more, and there was a general expectation that German and French recovery would restore a recognizable multistate system. Seen from Tokyo, however, the situation in Northeast Asia held no such promise. Mr. Yoshida and Mr. Ashida seem to have given very little weight to China, despite its status as one of the Big Five. For them, the only powers that counted militarily were the United States and the Soviet Union.

In 1945–46, when they tried to plan Japan's future course on the assumption of continued American-Soviet collaboration, the prospects were dim. They saw that under such circumstances, even though a formal peace treaty were concluded, Japan's fate would be likely to remain entirely in the hands of one or both of the superpowers, who would be free to intervene directly in Japanese internal affairs, to regulate Japanese foreign trade and economic activity, and even perhaps further to diminish Japanese national territory. For if the United States and the Soviet Union had agreed to make a joint policy in the Far East, they would have constituted a duumvirate against whose judgment there would have been no appeal. And even if, as was more likely, they had been able to agree upon clearly delineated spheres of control, the result would not have been much better. For as long as they remained content with the agreed-upon division, each would have been potentially an absolute ruler in its sphere. Japan would have had no bargaining power and no room for maneuvering vis-à-vis either the United States or the Soviet Union. Thus, as Prime Minister Yoshida makes clear in his memoirs, the idea of declaring Japan's permanent neutrality and obtaining a territorial guarantee from the United States, Great Britain, the Soviet Union, and China was a proposal for making the best of a seemingly hopeless situation.

When events during 1946–47 in Korea, Poland, Germany, and in Tokyo itself raised the possibility of a United States–Soviet rivalry, Mr. Yoshida and Mr. Ashida were quick to recognize the opportunity, as well as the danger, which such a falling-out held for Japan. They assumed that if the superpowers were to become rivals, they would need allies. Allies, however dependent and vulnerable, possess a certain value. They hoped that the Japanese Government could translate that value into bargaining power, which in turn would give to Japan a measure of independence. In short, a United States–Soviet rivalry seemed to make possible for Japan a continued existence in a multistate system of sorts—an existence in which Japan could retain at least vestiges of sovereignty, if not the full power to make war and peace.

The choice of the United States as an ally was almost foregone. Not only were American troops occupying Japan, but Mr. Yoshida and Mr. Ashida had been opposed all through the 1930s to war with the United States. This opposition, which resulted in their leaving the Government several years before Pearl Harbor, was not entirely a matter of ideology. It also stemmed from their strategic view, which was that the United States was Japan's most dangerous enemy and most desirable ally—that the success of Japan's policy on the Asian continent, and the safety of the Empire, depended not simply on avoiding war with the United States but on cooperation with it. They were, it seems, convinced as early as the 1920s and the 1930s that the United States could build a navy strong enough to deprive Japan of access to the seas, and they believed that American resources and trade were essential to Japan's economic well-being.

Following the Pacific War, this view was more applicable than ever. To Mr. Yoshida and Mr. Ashida, it seemed obvious that American naval and air power could protect Japan from the Soviet Union and ensure its access to world trade. The Soviet Union, on the other hand, although occupying the northern islands within sight of Hokkaido and posing a real threat to Japan's security, appeared to be a continental land power, incapable of protecting the Japanese islands against the United States or ensuring Japan the means of economic survival.

III

MOREOVER, THIS STUDY suggests that while the Japanese Government was quick to see that for Japan a bit of cold war might not be such a bad thing, the Government also realized that a United States–Soviet rivalry involved great dangers. Most apparent at first was the danger that the United States Government might fail to see Japan's value as an ally, and that the alliance upon which all depended might not materialize. The reception given the Ashida memorandum in 1947, and the views expressed in Tokyo by Secretary of the Army Kenneth C. Royall in 1949, made this danger seem very real.

By 1951, however, a second and more serious menace was visible. It seemed terrifyingly possible that the United States and the Soviet Union might slip beyond propaganda struggles and diplomatic wrangling, beyond war by proxy, and precipitate themselves into a cataclysmic total war, in which Japan would be a battleground. Prime Minister Yoshida seems to have become seriously concerned during the 1951 Security Treaty negotiations that the United States Government was overreacting to the Communist victory in China and to the war in Korea; that in Special Ambassador Dulles' brand of militant anticommunism, and in his zeal to protect the Free World by means of regional military alliances, there was a serious danger that the Americans might provoke an avoidable showdown with the Russians in Northeast Asia.

The evidence concerning Prime Minister Yoshida's thinking on this point is not complete. But it is clear that he refused to agree to Ambassador Dulles' plans for a rearmed Japan and for military cooperation with the United States to protect the security of Asia. He argued that Japan's economy and morale made rearmament impossible. He also seems to have believed, however, that the Soviet threat to Japan was not great enough to warrant large-scale Japanese rearmament or a regional military pact. And it also seems clear from Japan's security treaty diplomacy and its limited rearmament through the 1950s and 1960s that the Government's policy has been to keep its security relationship with the United States as unprovocative and inoffensive as possible vis-à-vis the Soviet Union. For the Government has never built forces which could pose a threat to the Soviets, nor has it ever entered into any regional military obligations. Instead, having gotten Japan a *de facto* guarantee for its external security in 1951 in the form of the United States forces in Japan, the Japanese leaders concentrated their efforts from that time on to gaining a veto over the use of those forces and having them reduced to a symbol of the American guarantee and to a rear echelon for the United Nations Command in Korea.

IV

JUDGING FROM the success of Japan's economic recovery and its rapid rate of economic growth, it is tempting to conclude that during the 1960s Japan developed a large enough economic base to enable the Government to build much more powerful forces than it did, and to take over the burden of its external defense from the United States. Quite apart from the question of public opposition to large-scale rearmament, however, the Japanese Government seems to have taken the view that there is no strategy in sight equal or superior to the present one which the larger forces they might build could serve.

As the strategic discussion in the previous chapter indicates, the defense planners still see Japan as caught between the superpowers, almost as vulnerable militarily and economically as in 1947. Despite Peking's nuclear missile program, the Government does not seem to think that Communist China will pose a serious external threat to Japan until at least the mid-1970s, unless the Sino-Soviet rift were suddenly to close. For China still does not have the naval and air forces to threaten Japan, and its missile forces are very small compared to the Soviet arsenal, which is more than offset by the American deterrent. Although Japan ranks third in Gross National Product in the world, the Japanese Government realizes that the United States and the Soviet Union are still far out in the lead economically. The Japanese defense planners know that Japan has the necessary economic and technological base to build a *force de frappe*. But most of them do not agree with General Gallois's strategy,[1] and none of them believe that Japan can afford to build a force of offensive missiles or an ABM system powerful enough to protect Japan against the Soviet or American nuclear arsenals.

The Government could probably buy conventional naval, air, and land forces strong enough to enable Japan single-handedly to repulse a Soviet conventional attack. But so long as the United States is committed to the defense of South Korea and seems likely to retain its naval and air superiority in the Western Pacific, such forces seem to the Japanese to be an unnecessary duplication of effort. Finally, the concern of the defense planners over the possibility of interdiction of Japan's maritime shipping indicates that the Government

1. The views prevailing in the Government on an independent nuclear force and the awareness of, and reaction to, General Gallois's ideas are presented in *Nihon no Anzen Hoshō, 1967*, pp. 13–18, and also in Saeki's "Ajia no Anzen to Nihon." A thoughtful Japanese proponent of a *force de frappe* is former General Doi Akio, who recently published his strategic views in *Shin Senryaku to Nihon.*

today is as keenly aware as Mr. Yoshida and Mr. Ashida were in the 1930s that: (1) Japan's economic survival depends on access to distant resources and markets (oil from the Persian Gulf, iron ore from Australia and India, timber from Canada, just to mention a few); and (2) Japan is still far from having the resources to build the naval and air forces required to protect this essential shipping in the event of a protracted war. Only American naval and air power seem capable of performing this mission.

As in 1947, Japan cannot defend itself against either of the superpowers. The United States can still defend Japan against the Soviet Union (and Communist China). No one can defend Japan against the United States. In short, despite greatly increased technological and industrial resources, it is still difficult for the Japanese Government to see a reasonable alternative to its present strategy and defense arrangements. The defense budget may, on occasion, appear embarrassingly tiny, but it buys the forces necessary to implement the present policy. Just as importantly, the Government believes that this small defense budget, by being small, contributes to the economic growth rate. The Government continues to minimize the proportion of resources allocated to national defense, in order to maximize the quantity of resources available in the future.

Why choose a new strategy and buy bigger forces now, when the old, inexpensive strategy remains the best available? Better instead to hang on to the old strategy, use the savings to build the Gross National Product as rapidly as possible, so that if and when in the future it becomes necessary to choose another strategy, there may be enough resources to buy a satisfactory replacement.

V

FINALLY, IN CONCLUSION, there are two points worth keeping in mind. First, from the point of view of Japan's leaders, their defense policy has not been an imposition on the United States. On the contrary, the Japanese Government has consistently held that its preservation of internal security, its commitment to share in Japan's external defense, and its willingness to furnish bases and logistical support for United States military operations in the Far East, and most especially in Korea, have significantly contributed to American security and have constituted an appropriate *quid pro quo* for a mutual Japanese-American security agreement.

Secondly, although the Governments of Prime Ministers Yoshida, Hatoyama, Kishi, Ikeda, and Sato have largely succeeded in practice in implementing the defense policy conceived in 1947, they have never explained the essentials of this policy to the Japanese people or gained their support for it, nor have they persuaded the Americans to give up entirely their efforts to make Japan into a militarily more powerful and active ally. The Conservatives have managed to steer their way between the domestic opposition and the vagaries of United States policy, but it is well to remember that Japan's present defense arrangements, despite two decades of success and stability, could be quickly rendered ineffective either by the Japanese voter or by a dramatic shift in American Far Eastern policy, most especially an American decision to withdraw from the defense of South Korea.

Appendix A: Security Treaty between the United States and Japan, September 8, 1951

Japan has this day signed a Treaty of Peace with the Allied Powers. On the coming into force of that Treaty, Japan will not have the effective means to exercise its inherent right of self-defense because it has been disarmed. There is danger to Japan in this situation because irresponsible militarism has not yet been driven from the world. Therefore, Japan desires a Security Treaty with the United States of America to come into force simultaneously with the Treaty of Peace between the United States of America and Japan. The Treaty of Peace recognizes that Japan as a sovereign nation has the right to enter into collective security arrangements, and further, the Charter of the United Nations recognizes that all nations possess an inherent right of individual and collective self-defense.

In exercise of these rights, Japan desires, as a provisional arrangement for its defense, that the United States of America should maintain armed forces of its own in and about Japan so as to deter armed attack upon Japan.

The United States of America, in the interest of peace and security, is presently willing to maintain certain of its armed forces in and about Japan, in the expectation, however, that Japan will itself increasingly assume responsibility for its own defense against direct and indirect aggression, always avoiding any armament which could be an offensive threat or serve other than to promote peace and security in accordance with the purposes and principles of the United Nations Charter.

Accordingly, the two countries have agreed as follows:

Article I. Japan grants, and the United States of America accepts the right, upon the coming into force of the Treaty of Peace and of this Treaty, to dispose United States land, air, and sea forces in and about Japan. Such forces may be utilized to contribute to the maintenance of the international peace and security in the Far East and to the security of Japan against armed attack from without, including assistance given at the express request of the Japanese Government to put down large-scale internal riots and disturbances in Japan, caused through instigation or intervention by an outside Power or Powers.

Article II. During the exercise of the right referred to in Article I, Japan will not grant, without the prior consent of the United States of America, any bases or any rights, power, or authority whatsoever, in or relating to bases or the right of garrison or of maneuver, or transit of ground, air, or naval forces to any third Power.

Article III. The conditions which shall govern the disposition of armed forces of the United States of America in and about Japan shall be determined by administrative agreements between the two Governments.

Article IV. This Treaty shall expire whenever in the opinion of the Governments of the United States of America and of Japan there shall have come into force such United Nations arrangements or such alternative individual or collective security dispositions as will satisfactorily provide for the maintenance by the United Nations or otherwise of international peace and security in the Japan Area.

Article V. This Treaty shall be ratified by the United States of America and Japan and will come into force when instruments of ratification thereof have been exchanged by them at Washington.

IN WITNESS WHEREOF the undersigned plenipotentiaries have signed this Treaty.

DONE in duplicate at the city of San Francisco, in the English and Japanese languages, this eighth day of September, 1951.

Appendix B: Treaty of Mutual Cooperation and Security between the United States and Japan, Signed at Washington, D.C., January 19, 1960

The United States of America and Japan,

Desiring to strengthen the bonds of peace and friendship traditionally existing between them, and to uphold the principles of democracy, individual liberty, and the rule of law,

Desiring further to encourage closer economic cooperation between them and to promote conditions of economic stability and well-being in their countries,

Reaffirming their faith in the purposes and principles of the Charter of the United Nations, and their desire to live in peace with all peoples and all governments,

Recognizing that they have the inherent right of individual or collective self-defense as affirmed in the Charter of the United Nations,

Considering that they have a common concern in the maintenance of international peace and security in the Far East,

Having resolved to conclude a treaty of mutual cooperation and security,

Therefore agree as follows:

Article I. The Parties undertake, as set forth in the Charter of the United Nations, to settle any international disputes in which they may be involved by peaceful means in such a manner that international peace and security and justice are not endangered and to refrain in their international relations from the threat or use of force against the territorial integrity or political independence of any state, or in any other manner inconsistent with the purposes of the United Nations.

The Parties will endeavor in concert with other peace-loving countries to strengthen the United Nations so that its mission of maintaining international peace and security may be discharged more effectively.

Article II. The Parties will contribute toward the further development of peaceful and friendly international relations by strengthening their free institutions, by bringing about a better understanding of the principles upon which these institutions are founded, and by promoting conditions of stability and well-being. They will seek to eliminate conflict in their international economic policies and will encourage economic collaboration between them.

Article III. The Parties, individually and in cooperation with each other, by means of continuous and effective self-help and mutual aid will maintain and develop, subject to their constitutional provisions, their capacities to resist armed attack.

Article IV. The Parties will consult together from time to time regarding the implementation of this Treaty, and, at the request of either Party, whenever the security of Japan or international peace and security in the Far East is threatened.

Article V. Each Party recognizes that an armed attack against either Party in the territories under the administration of Japan would be dangerous to its own peace and safety and declares that it would act to meet the common danger in accordance with its constitutional provisions and processes.

Any such armed attack and all measures taken as a result thereof shall be immediately reported to the Security Council of the United Nations in accordance with the provisions of Article 51 of the Charter. Such measures shall be terminated when the Security Council has taken the measures necessary to restore and maintain international peace and security.

Article VI. For the purpose of contributing to the security of Japan and the maintenance of international peace and security in the Far East, the United States of America is granted the use by its land, air, and naval forces of facilities and areas in Japan.

The use of these facilities and areas as well as the status of the United States armed forces in Japan shall be governed by a separate agreement, replacing the administrative Agreement under Article III of the Security Treaty between the United States of America and Japan, signed at Tokyo on February 28, 1952, as amended, and by such other arrangements as may be agreed upon.

Article VII. This Treaty does not affect and shall not be interpreted as affecting in any way the rights and obligations of the Parties under the Charter of the United Nations or the responsibility of the United Nations for the maintenance of international peace and security.

Article VIII. This Treaty shall be ratified by the United States of America and Japan in accordance with their respective constitutional processes and will enter into force on the date on which the instruments of ratification thereof have been exchanged by them in Tokyo.

Article IX. The Security Treaty between the United States of America and Japan signed at the city of San Francisco on September 8, 1951, shall expire upon the entering into force of this Treaty.

Article X. This Treaty shall remain in force until in the opinion of the Governments of the United States of America and Japan there shall have come into force such United Nations arrangements as will satisfactorily provide for the maintenance of international peace and security in the Japan area.

However, after the Treaty has been in force for ten years, either Party may give notice to the other Party of its intention to terminate the Treaty, in which case the Treaty shall terminate one year after such notice has been given.

IN WITNESS WHEREOF the undersigned Plenipotentiaries have singed this Treaty.

DONE in duplicate at Washington in the English and Japanese languages, both equally authentic, this 19th day of January, 1960.

Bibliography

OFFICIAL DOCUMENTS

Japan. *Bōei Jitsumu Shoroppō, 1967*. Tokyo: Naigai Shuppan Sha, 1968.

—— *Jieitai Jūnen Shi*. Tokyo: Okurasho Insatsu Kyoku, 1961.

—— Sangiin Iin Kaigi Roku.

—— Shugiin Iin Kaigi Roku.

Union of Soviet Socialist Republics. Ministry of Foreign Affairs. *Stalin's Correspondence with Roosevelt and Truman, 1941–1945*. New York: Capricorn Books, 1965.

United Nations. Secretariat. *United Nations Treaty Series*.

United States. Arms Control and Disarmament Agency. *World Wide Military Expenditures and Related Data, Calendar Year 1965*.

—— Congress. Senate. Committee on Foreign Relations. *Treaty of Mutual Cooperation and Security with Japan*. 86th Congress, 2d Session, 1960.

—— Department of State. *American Foreign Policy, 1950–1955: Basic Documents*. Vol. II, 1957.

—— Department of State. *Bulletin*.

—— Department of State. *United States Treaties and Other International Agreements*.

—— Headquarters, United States Forces Japan. *United States–Japan Treaties, Agreements and Other Documents*. May 1, 1961.

—— Supreme Commander for the Allied Powers. *Political Reorientation of Japan: September 1945 to September 1948*. 2 vols. Washington, D.C.: G.P.O., 1949.

—— Supreme Commander for the Allied Powers. *Summation of Non-Military Activities in Japan*. February, 1947.

BOOKS, ARTICLES, AND OTHER PRINTED SOURCES

Allen, G. C. *Japan's Economic Recovery.* London: Oxford University Press, 1958.

American Embassy, Tokyo. *Daily Summary of the Japanese Press.*
—— *Summaries of Selected Japanese Magazines.*

Asahi Nenkan. 1947–1968. Tokyo: Asahi Shimbun Sha.

Asahi Shimbun. *Jieitai.* Tokyo: Asahi Shimbun Sha, 1968.
—— *Soren Gaikō to Ajia.* Tokyo: Asahi Shimbun Sha, 1967.

Baerwald, Hans. *The Purge of Japanese Leaders under the Occupation.* Berkeley: University of California Press, 1959.

Ball, William Macmahon. *Japan—Enemy or Ally?* New York: John Day & Company, 1949.

Bell, Coral. "Korea and the Balance of Power," *The Political Quarterly,* XXV (January–March, 1954), 17–29.

Beloff, Max. *Soviet Policy in the Far East, 1944–1951.* London: Oxford University Press, 1953.

Bisson, T. A. *Zaibatsu Dissolution in Japan.* Berkeley: University of California Press, 1954.

Bōei Nenkan. 1955–68. Tokyo: Bōei Nenkan Kankō Kai.

Borton, Hugh. *Japan's Modern Century.* New York: The Ronald Press, 1955.

Buck, James H. "The Japanese Self-Defense Forces," *Asian Survey* (September, 1967), pp. 597–613.

Bull, Hedley. "Strategic Studies and Its Critics," *World Politics,* XX (July, 1968), 593–605.

Butow, Robert J. C. *Tojo and the Coming of the War.* Princeton: Princeton University Press, 1961.

Clark, Mark W. *From the Danube to the Yalu.* New York: Harper and Brothers, 1954.

Coox, Alvin D., and Yoshitaka Horie. "Japan's Self Defense Force Today," *Marine Corps Gazette* (February, 1965), pp. 50–53.

Council on Foreign Relations. *The United States in World Affairs, 1949–1962.* Ed. R. P. Stebbins. New York: Harper and Row.

Crowley, James B. *Japan's Quest for Autonomy.* Princeton: Princeton University Press, 1966.

Curtis, Gerald L. "Dulles-Yoshida Negotiations," in *Columbia Essays in International Affairs.* Vol. II. New York: Columbia University Press, 1967.

Doba Hajime. *Nihon no Gunji Ryoku.* Tokyo: Yomiuri Shimbun Sha, 1963.

Doba Hajime *et al. Bōeichō*. Tokyo: Meibun Sha, 1956.

Doi Akio. *Shin Senryaku to Nihon*. Tokyo: Jiji Tsushin Sha, 1968.

Etō Shinkichi *et al.* "Sekai Senryaku to Nihon no Anzen Koso," *Gendai no Me* (Tokushu) (August, 1967), pp. 89–101.

Feis, Herbert. *Contest over Japan*. New York: W. W. Norton and Company, 1967.

—— *The Road to Pearl Harbor*. Princeton: Princeton University Press, 1950.

Figges, J. F. "The Japanese Armed Forces," *Japan Society of London Bulletin*, No. 36 (February, 1962), pp. 2–4.

Fujiwara Akira. "Sanji Bō to Gunji Ryoku no Shin Kaidan," *Sekai* (June, 1967), pp. 125–33.

Fujiwara Hirotatsu and Tomita Nobuo. *Hoshu Dokusai no Teihen*. Tokyo: Bungadō Ginkō Kenkyūsha, 1968.

Haji Fumiō. *Ningen Ikeda Hayato*. Tokyo: Noma Shōichi, 1967.

Herz, John H. *International Politics in the Atomic Age*. New York: Columbia University Press, 1963.

Hitch, Charles J., and Roland M. McKean. *The Economics of Defense in the Nuclear Age*. New York: Atheneum Press, 1965.

Hitchcock, Wilbur H. "North Korea Jumps the Gun," *Current History*, XX, No. 115 (March, 1951), 136–44.

Hoffman, Stanley. *The State of War*. New York: Frederick A. Praeger, 1965.

Hokugo Gentarō (pseudonym). "Kaihara Kambocho no Seppuku," *Gunji Kenkyū* (November, 1966), pp. 132–37.

Hoshino Yasusaburo. *Jieitai-Sono Futatsu no Men*. Tokyo: Sanichi Sho Bo, 1963.

Huntington, Samuel P. *The Common Defense*. New York: Columbia University Press, 1961.

Ike, Nobutaka, ed. and trans. *Japan's Decision for War: Records of the 1941 Policy Conferences*. Stanford: Stanford University Press, 1967.

The Japan Statistical Yearbook. Tokyo: The Prime Minister's Office.

Jiminto Anzen Hoshō Chōsa Kai. *Nihon no Anzen to Bōei*. Tokyo: Izumi Sho Bō, 1966.

Jones, Francis C. *Japan's New Order in East Asia*. London: Oxford University Press, 1954.

Kamimura Shinichi. *Sōgō Kyōryoku Anzen Hoshō Jōyaku no Kaisetsu*. Tokyo: Jiji Shin Sha, 1965.

Kawada Tadashi. "Seichō Suru Nihon no Bōei Sangyō," *Sekai* (October, 1964), pp. 64–74.

Kawai, Kazuo. *Japan's American Interlude*. Chicago: University of Chicago Press, 1960.

Kennan, George F. "Japanese Security and American Policy," *Foreign Affairs*, XLIII, No. 1 (October, 1964), 14–28.

—— *Memoirs, 1925–1950*. Boston: Little, Brown and Company, 1967.

Kichi Miyazawa. *Tōkyō-Washington no Mitsudan*. Tokyo: Jitsugyo no Hi Sha, 1956.

Kishida Junnosuke *et al*. *Chūgoku no Kaku Sen Ryoku*. Tokyo: Asahi Shimbun Sha, 1967.

Kobayashi Naoki. *Nihon ni Okeru Kempō Dōtai no Bunseki*. Tokyo: Iwanami, 1963.

Kobayashi Tatsuo. "Kaigun Mondai," *Taiheiyō Sensō e no Michi*. Vol. I. Tokyo: Asahi Shimbun Sha, 1962.

Kōsaka Masataka. *Saishō Yoshida Shigeru*. Tokyo: Chuo Koron Sha, 1968.

—— "Saishō Yoshida Shigeru Ron," *Chūō Kōron* (February, 1965), pp. 102–27.

Kotani Hidejirō and Tanaka Naokichi. *Nihon no Anzen Hoshō*. Tokyo: Kajima Kenkyū Jo Shuppankai, 1964.

Kurahara Nobuhiro. *Nichi-Bei Ampō Jōyaku no Shōten*. Tokyo: Asahi Shimbun Sha, 1967.

MacArthur, Douglas. *Reminiscences*. New York: McGraw-Hill Book Company, 1964.

McNelly, Theodore. "The Renunciation of War in the Japanese Constitution," *Political Science Quarterly*, LXXVII, No. 3 (September, 1962), 350–78.

Maeda Hisashi. *Nihon no Bōei Seisaku*. Asahi Shimbun Sha Anzen Hoshō Mondai Chōsa Kai 20. July 1, 1967.

Maki, John M., ed. *Conflict and Tension in the Far East: Key Documents, 1894–1960*. Seattle: University of Washington Press, 1961.

—— *Court and Constitution in Japan: Selected Supreme Court Decisions, 1948–1960*. Seattle: University of Washington Press, 1964.

Matsueda, Tsukasa, and George Moore. "Japan's Shifting Attitude Toward the Military: Mitsuya Kenkyu and the Self-Defense Forces," *Asian Survey* (September, 1967), pp. 614–25.

Maxon, Yale C. *Control of Japanese Foreign Policy*. Berkeley: University of California Press, 1957.

Mendel, Douglas H. *The Japanese People and Foreign Policy.* Berkeley: University of California Press, 1961.

Morgenthau, Hans J. *Politics among Nations.* New York: Alfred A. Knopf, 1954.

Morley, James W. *Japan and Korea, America's Allies in the Pacific.* New York: Walker and Company, 1965.

—— "Japan's Security Policy in Transition," *Current History* (April, 1964), pp. 200–6.

Murphy, Robert D. *Diplomat among Warriors.* Garden City: Doubleday and Company, 1964.

Nagai Yōnosuke. "Japanese Foreign Policy Objectives in a Nuclear Milieu," *Journal of Social and Political Ideas in Japan,* V, No. 1 (April, 1967), 27–42.

Nihon Kyōsantō. *Nihon Kyōsantō no Susumu Michi.* Tokyo: Nihon Kyōsantō Shuppan Bu, 1948.

Nihon no Anzen Hoshō. 1966–67. Tokyo: Anzen Hoshō Chōsa Kai.

"Nihon no Bōei—Anata wa Dore o Erabu," *Shūkan Asahi* (April 5, 1968), pp. 22–37.

Nishimura Kumao. *Anzen Hoshō Jōyaku Ron.* Tokyo: Jiji Tsushin Sha, 1959.

—— "Nichi Bei Anzen Hoshō Jōyaku no Seiritsu Jijō," in Kotani Hidejirō and Tanaka Naokichi, eds., *Nihon no Anzen Hoshō.* Tokyo: Kajima Shuppan Kai, 1964.

Nozaka Sanzō. *Senryaku, Senjutsu no Shomondai.* Tokyo: Obei Shobo, 1948.

Packard, George R., III. *Protest in Tokyo.* Princeton: Princeton University Press, 1966.

Reischauer, Edwin O. *The United States and Japan.* New York: The Viking Press, 1962.

Rōyama Michio. "Kaku Senryaku no Igi to Nihon no Shōrai," *Chūō Kōron* (March, 1968), pp. 50–67.

Saeki Kiichi. "Ajia no Anzen to Nihon," *Kyokutō no Anzen Hoshō,* pp. 9–36. Tokyo: Izumi Sho Bo, 1968.

—— *Nihon no Anzen Hoshō.* Tokyo: Nihon Kokusai Mondai Kenkyū Jo, 1966.

Sakanaka Tomohisa *et al. Nihon no Jiei Ryoku.* Tokyo: Asahi Shimbun Sha, 1967.

Shinobu Seizaburo. *Ampō Tōsō Shi.* Tokyo: Sekai Shoin, 1961.

—— *Sengo Nihon Seiji Shi.* 4 vols. Tokyo: Jiji Tsushin Sha, 1967.

Stockwin, Arthur. *The Japanese Socialist Party and Neutralism.* London: Cambridge University Press, 1968.

Sugita Ichiji. *Wasurarete Iru Anzen Hoshō.* Tokyo: Jiji Tsushin Sha, 1967.

Swearingen, Roger, and Paul F. Langer. *Red Flag in Japan.* Cambridge, Mass.: Harvard University Press, 1952.

Takeuchi Iwaō, ed. *Yoshida Naikaku.* Tokyo: Yoshida Naikaku Kanko Kai, 1954.

Tanaka Naokichi. *Kaku Jidai no Nihon no Anzen Hoshō.* Tokyo: Kajima Kenkyū Jo Shuppankai, 1966.

—— *Nihon Bōei ni Kansuru 12 Sho.* Tokyo: Nihon Shin Sho, 1965.

—— *See also* Kotani Hidejirō.

Tatsumi Teruichi. "Saigunbi to Yoshida-san no Gankosa," in Yoshida Shigeru, *Kaisō Jūnen*, III, 180–81. Tokyo: Shin Shio Sha, 1957.

"Third Defense Program and the Munitions Industry," *The Oriental Economist* (June, 1967), pp. 354–61.

Truman, Harry S. *Memoirs.* 2 vols. Garden City: Doubleday and Company, 1955.

Van Aduard, E. J. Lewe. *Japan from Surrender to Peace.* New York: Frederick A. Praeger, 1954.

Ward, Robert E. *The Position of Japan in the Far East and in International Politics, 1965–70.* Santa Barbara: General Electric Company, Technical Military Planning Operation, 1958.

Weinstein, Martin E. "Defending Postwar Japan," *The New Leader* (July 3, 1967), pp. 12–15.

—— "Japanese Air Self-Defense Force—Restrained but Powerful," *Air Force Space Digest* (December, 1967), pp. 56–63.

Whitney, Courtney. *MacArthur: His Rendezvous with History.* New York: Alfred A. Knopf, 1956.

Wildes, Harry Emerson. *Typhoon in Tokyo.* New York: The Macmillan Company, 1954.

Willoughby, Charles A., and John Chamberlain. *MacArthur: 1941–1945.* New York: McGraw-Hill Book Company, 1954.

Yoshida Shigeru. *Kaisō Jūnen.* 4 vols. Tokyo: Shin Shio Sha, 1957.

—— *The Yoshida Memoirs.* Trans. Yoshida Kenichi. Boston: Houghton Mifflin Company, 1962.

"Yoshida Shigeru ga Kataru Gaikō Hiwa" [transcript of NHK television interview, August 29, 1965], *Heibon Panchi* (September 20, 1965), pp. 7–31.

UNPUBLISHED MATERIALS

Eichelberger, Robert L. Unpublished diary. Manuscript Department, William R. Perkins Library, Duke University.

Kokubō Kaigi. Kambō Kyoku. "Waga Kuni Bōei Ryoku no Kihon to Bōei Ryoku Seibi no Arikata." October, 1966.

Letter, dated August 22, 1968, from Clovis E. Byers, Lieutenant General, U.S. Army, Retired, former Eighth Army Chief of Staff.

Weinstein, Martin E. "The Rebuilding of Japan's Armed Forces." Unpublished Master's Thesis. Department of Public Law and Government and East Asian Institute, Columbia University, 1965.

INTERVIEWS

Mr. Hata Ikuhiko, Faculty, National Defense College. July 8, November 4, 1967, April 19, 1968.

Mr. Kaihara Osamu, secretary-general, National Defense Council. April 2 and June 5, 1968.

Mr. Kishida Junnosuke, Asahi Newspaper Security Policy Research Council. September 12, December 3, 1967, April 29, 1968.

Mr. Kōtani Hidejirō, professor of international politics, Kyoto Industrial University. July 28, 1967.

Mr. Matsumoto Shigeharu, editor of Yoshida Shigeru's *Kaisō Jūnen.* June 7 and 10, 1968.

Mr. Momoi Makoto, Faculty, National Defense College. August 3, 1967, February 7, April 18, 1968.

Mr. Robert D. Murphy, former United States ambassador to Japan. October 31, 1968.

Mr. Nishimura Kumao, former chief, Treaty Bureau, Foreign Ministry. March 13, 1968.

Mr. Noda Hidejirō, Foreign Ministry, Asian Affairs Bureau, Northeast Asia Section Chief. May 10, 1968.

Mr. Saeki Kiichi, former commandant, National Defense College. August 29, 1967.

Mr. Sakanaka Tomohisa, Asahi Newspaper, Political Section. December 5, 1967, April 12, May 16, 19, 1968.

Mr. Sezaki Kasami and Mr. Yoshida Shigenobu, Foreign Ministry, North American Affairs Bureau, Security Treaty Section. April 25, May 7, 1968.

Mr. Suzuki Tadakatsu, former director, Central Liaison Agency. March 1, 1968.

Mr. Wakaizumi Kei, professor of international politics, Kyoto Industrial University, October 16, 1967.

Mr. Yasuda Hiro, chief, Legal Section, Defense Agency, April 4, 1968.

Mr. Yoshida Kenichi, translator of *Kaisō Jūnen*. June 6, 1968. (Interview by telephone.)

Index

Acheson, Dean: and peace settlement, 21–22, 25; Far Eastern policy, 47n; and Yoshida, notes, 52, 99

Aiken, George D., 97

Air Self-Defense Force, 75, 109, 110, 113; see also Self-Defense Forces

Akagi Munenori, 120, 121

Aleutian Islands, 47

Allied Council for Japan, 18n

Allison, John M., 81, 86, 95

Anti-Police Law Revision Movement, 91

Ashida Hitoshi, 10, 11, 19, 129, 130; opposed to war with U.S., 10, 130; Soviet threat to peace and security, 10, 21, 22, 26, 27, 31, 40–41, 105, 106; memorandum on defense, 24–28, 31, 39–40, 41, 43, 44, 45, 46, 56, 58, 62, 63, 66, 69, 87, 101, 105, 128, 131; on Security Treaty (1951), 43, 54n, 56; on rearmament, 54n; ill feeling toward Yoshida over security negotiations, 54n, 60n; sees neutrality as impractical, 105

Atcheson, George, 14, 18–19, 22; wants security guarantee for Japan from the United Nations, 19, 20

Atomic and nuclear weapons, 80–83, 86, 95, 98, 102, 112, 115, 133

Australia: troops in Japan, 29; see also Commonwealth

Ball, William Macmahon, 18n, 37

Bonin Islands, 5; Japanese sovereignty and claims, 6, 15, 92, 93; U.S. forces, 7, 27, 44, 92–93, 105; Japanese concern over defense, 92–93, 94

Borton, Dr. Hugh, 19

Byers, Clovis E., 24n

Byrnes, James, 19

China, 7–8, 129; policy toward Japan, 5–6; civil war, 6, 10, 46; as member of Allied Council for Japan, 18n; favors Big Four conference on peace, 23

China, Communist, 46; as possible threat to Japan, 41n–42n, 112, 114, 115, 117, 129, 133; Korean War, 46; military alliance with USSR, 46, 47; Yoshida on, 49

China, Nationalist, 46–47, 47–48

Clark, Mark W., 70, 71, 72–73

Cohen, Theodore, 38

Commonwealth: as member of Allied Council for Japan, 18n; favors eleven-nation peace con-

Studies of the East Asian Institute

The Ladder of Success in Imperial China, by Ping-ti Ho. New York: Columbia University Press, 1962; reprint, John Wiley, 1964.

The Chinese Inflation, 1937–1949, by Shun-hsin Chou. New York: Columbia University Press, 1963.

Reformer in Modern China: Chang Chien, 1853–1926, by Samuel Chu. New York: Columbia University Press, 1965.

Research in Japanese Sources: A Guide, by Herschel Webb with the assistance of Marleigh Ryan. New York: Columbia University Press, 1965.

Society and Education in Japan, by Herbert Passin. New York: Bureau of Publications, Teachers College, Columbia University, 1965.

Agricultural Production and Economic Development in Japan, 1873–1922, by James I. Nakamura. Princeton: Princeton University Press, 1966.

Japan's First Modern Novel: Ukigumo of Futabatei Shimei, by Marleigh Ryan. New York: Columbia University Press, 1967.

The Korean Communist Movement, 1918–1948, by Dae-sook Suh. Princeton: Princeton University Press, 1967.

The First Vietnam Crisis, by Melvin Gurtov. New York: Columbia University Press, 1967.

Cadres, Bureaucracy, and Political Power in Communist China, by A. Doak Barnett. New York: Columbia University Press, 1967.

The Japanese Imperial Institution in the Tokugawa Period, by Herschel Webb. New York: Columbia University Press, 1968.

The Recruitment of University Graduates in Big Firms in Japan, by Koya Azumi. New York: Teachers College Press, Columbia University, 1968.

The Communists and Chinese Peasant Rebellion: A Study in the Rewriting of Chinese History, by James P. Harrison, Jr. New York: Atheneum Publishers, 1969.

How the Conservatives Rule Japan, by Nathaniel B. Thayer. Princeton: Princeton University Press, 1969.

Aspects of Chinese Education, edited by C. T. Hu. New York: Teachers College Press, Columbia University, 1969.

Economic Development and the Labor Market in Japan, by Koji Taira. New York: Columbia University Press, 1970.

The Japanese Oligarchy and the Russo-Japanese War, by Shumpei Okamoto. New York: Columbia University Press, 1970.

Documents on Korean Communism, by Dae-sook Suh. Princeton: Princeton University Press, 1970.

Japan's Postwar Defense Policy, 1947–1968, by Martin E. Weinstein. New York: Columbia University Press, 1971.

Imperial Restoration in Medieval Japan, by H. Paul Varley. New York: Columbia University Press (forthcoming).

Li Tsung-jen: A Memoir, edited by T. K. Tong. Berkeley: University of California Press (forthcoming).